KSHITIJ TIWARI

The PhD Scholar's Compass

From burnout to breakthrough

First edition

ISBN (paperback): 978-93-5469-239-0
ISBN (hardcover): 978-93-5469-490-5

This book was professionally typeset on Reedsy.
Find out more at reedsy.com

For my parents.
To my mother, whose dedication to her students taught me that success is the true reward.
To my father, who showed me the power of applying academic knowledge to real-world problems and communicating with empathy.
Your examples have been my first compass. This book reflects the values you instilled in me.
And to every scholar navigating their own wilderness—may this compass light your path.

The PhD is neither a marathon of steady endurance nor a single sprint of genius; it is a meticulously planned series of high-intensity sprints, demanding strategic recovery and unwavering psychological defense between each one.

Kshitij Tiwari, Ph.D.

Contents

Foreword

Every so often, a book comes along that feels larger than its title. *The PhD Scholar's Compass* by **Dr. Kshitij Tiwari** presents itself as a resource for doctoral aspirants, yet what it offers is a far more universal guide for anyone navigating a demanding professional journey and seeking clarity in the midst of complexity.

I have had the privilege of interacting with Dr. Tiwari for several years through our exchanges on engineering and innovation on LinkedIn. Even in those brief interactions, his clarity of thought and his ability to confront difficult questions with honesty have always stood out. This book reflects those qualities deeply.

Dr. Tiwari does not simply provide a roadmap; he offers a compass. The PhD journey, as he describes, is not a linear path with predictable milestones, but a landscape filled with unmarked trails, shifting expectations, and silent pressures. What makes this guide exceptional is its commitment to addressing not only the intellectual demands of research but also the emotional and psychological realities—burnout, imposter syndrome, unspoken academic norms, and the culture that shapes a scholar's identity.

And yet, the relevance goes far beyond academia. The frameworks, reflections, and practical tools in these chapters apply to any professional striving for excellence in a high-stakes environment. Whether one is in research, engineering, entrepreneurship, or industry, the need for resilience, purpose, and adaptability remains the same.

This book offers what many professionals seek but rarely find: actionable templates, honest insights, and a holistic understanding of what it means to pursue a challenging goal while staying grounded, healthy, and self-aware.

For some readers, these pages will confirm their passion for doctoral research. For others, they may illuminate an entirely different path. In either case, this book serves exactly as intended—a compass pointing toward clarity, growth, and meaningful choice.

I invite you to read it thoughtfully and discover the lessons that extend far beyond the pursuit of a PhD.

— *Daniel Christadoss*

Preface

The compass of your PhD journey is not a tool to find a pre-existing well-tread cookie-cutter path, but the instrument that teaches you to trust your own sense of direction through the wilderness.
-Kshitij Tiwari, PhD

The PhD Scholar's Compass: From Burnout to Breakthrough

A self-help guide for PhD scholars

Welcome, PhD aspirant. Whether you are aspiring to sign up for a PhD or are already in program, you are likely seeking a map to guide you to the destination- the PhD finish line or in social media lingo, #PhDdone. Instead, you're holding a **compass, not a map**. And you must be wondering why the compass?

A PhD journey isn't a straight line from point A to point B; it is an expedition through dense, often-unmarked territory. The traditional academic world gives you a powerful flashlight—your research and inquisitive skills—but it rarely provides a guide for the emotional and mental whirlwind you'll inevitably encounter.

This book is that guide, the companion every early-stage PhD scholar needs. It's written for anyone navigating the complex landscape of doctoral studies—from the first-year student to the candidate in the final stretch. It's born from two decades of navigating academia's highs and lows, mentoring countless students across a myriad of education systems, and seeing firsthand the silent struggles that no one talks about. We'll cover the unwritten rules, the unspoken expectations, and the real-world strategies that textbooks and professors just don't teach. This is a guide for moving from simply surviving to **truly thriving**, transforming your PhD from a source of stress into a powerful journey of personal and professional growth.

This guide goes beyond simple advice. What makes it unique is its commitment to providing **detailed, actionable resources**. Unlike other books that only tell you *what* to do, this guide gives you the tools to actually do it. Throughout the chapters, you will find **specific templates for challenging conversations**, step-by-step guides for mastering difficult academic tasks, and structured frameworks for turning abstract ideas into concrete action. This book is a practical toolkit designed to be used, not just read, taking you from PhD burnout to breakthrough, one chapter at a time.

In addition to these resources, this guide stands apart by focusing on three critical, often-overlooked aspects of the PhD journey. **First**, we tackle the **unwritten rules of academic culture**, demystifying the power dynamics and unspoken expectations that can leave even the most brilliant students feeling lost. **Second**, we prioritize your **holistic well-being** as a researcher, addressing the profound psychological challenges like burnout and imposter syndrome as central components of the experience, not just as side notes. **Finally**, we look **beyond the degree** to help you understand and articulate the transferable skills you are building, preparing you for a successful career both inside and outside of academia. These unique aspects are designed to provide a comprehensive and honest roadmap for your journey.

Prologue

I started my PhD journey abroad with a clear and certain destination: success. Like many, I held a romanticized vision of a linear progression, imagining a clean, upward trajectory of intellectual breakthrough and professional advancement. The reality, however, was a brutal ambush.

The first year was a blur of logistics—the grueling applications, the culture shock, the endless questions about "What do I consider?" and "How do I account for my family's reservations?" But the true earthquake hit later. Just as the rhythm of research began to take hold, my world came to a halt with the sudden loss of someone very dear to me.

I found myself standing at a forked road—one path was a desperate return home; the other, an unbearable continuation of the work. The clarity, the motivation, the sheer will to keep going were completely annihilated. I was professionally stuck and personally hollowed out, staring into the academic wilderness with no map and no light.

In the midst of that profound turmoil, a quiet voice cut through the noise: my mother's lifelong counsel.

> "Finish what you start, and don't start what you can't finish."

It was a simple, grounding principle. It didn't tell me where to go, but it taught me how to **trust the compass** inside me. It gave me the strength to rebuild my resolve, one difficult day at a time.

This journey revealed the most profound challenge of the PhD: the problem isn't just the research—it's **finding the critical alignment** between your own working style and your advisor's supervision style to help you compound your efforts.

This book, ***The PhD Scholar's Compass***, is the product of everything I learned in that wilderness. It offers you the concrete templates and strategies to find your own professional alignment, move from *burnout to breakthrough*, and build a career based on integrity and lasting purpose.

This compass is for you, my fellow scholar.

May it light your path and lead you home.

I

Orienting your compass – Understanding the PhD terrain

The PhD demands professional rigor, not just intellectual curiosity. This Part sets your trajectory by defining your core motivation, strategically selecting the right university, executing effective cold outreach, thoroughly vetting your future supervisor, decoding the unwritten rules of academic culture, and completing your mental and logistical launch preparation. We move from romantic myth to actionable strategy, ensuring you are ready before you step onto campus.

1

Is PhD right for you?

The PhD is often called a marathon not a sprint, but, in reality, it is neither. So, what is it then? It is a **series of sprints**—intense, focused bursts of effort followed by periods of recovery and strategic planning. But even this is too neat. A PhD is more like volunteering to live in a dense fog sustained for years, where the path changes daily, the finish line is invisible, and only one person—you—can provide the motivation to keep walking. You have to be your own cheerleader.

This chapter should be the most uncomfortable, yet most honest, read of this entire book. Before you begin the tactical work of applications and networking, you must pause and confront the single most overlooked question: **Is PhD the right choice for me?**

The great oversight: Why scholars skip introspection

Many future scholars glide into the PhD process driven not by a powerful internal compass, but by external inertia. You've been successful in high school, then Undergraduate, then the Master's program. The next logical, expected step is the doctorate. The application is a bureaucratic obstacle, not an existential one. However, this necessary commitment requires a personal audit—a deep introspection—that most scholars neglect.

Skipping this self-evaluation is the primary reason for burnout, disillusionment, and attrition five years down the line. It plants your foundation on borrowed purpose, not inherent passion. So, how does one tell apart the wrong and right reasons for pursuing a PhD?

The wrong reasons: Motivations that fail

Pursuing a PhD for the wrong reasons is a guarantee of future misery. These motivations are unsustainable because they focus on what the degree *represents* rather than what the *work requires.*

The traps of unsound motivation:

- **The status trap:** *"I want the title 'Dr.' and the prestige."* Prestige is fleeting and does not help you write 80,000 words. The daily reality of PhD life involves frustration, failure, and isolation, none of which feel prestigious.

- **The job avoidance trap:** *"I don't know what else to do, so*

I'll defer the real world." A PhD is not a four-year time-out; it is intense, focused labor. It amplifies, not defers, responsibility.

- **The life deferral trap:** *"I need an acceptable excuse to postpone real-life challenges (like family planning or settling down)."* The all-consuming, long-term academic commitment provides a convenient, socially acceptable shield against difficult personal conversations and societal pressures. Using the PhD as a form of escapism is a recipe for deep personal resentment later.

- **The pressure trap:** *"My parents/mentor/society expects this of me."* External approval is a terrible fuel source for an internal fire. When the stress hits, you will resent the people whose expectations you are fulfilling, not motivate yourself to continue.

- **The salary trap:** *"This degree guarantees a high-paying job."* In many fields, a PhD is necessary to reach the top research positions, but the years spent earning it (often at a low stipend) and the opportunity costs often make this a poor financial decision compared to entering the industry sooner. The motivation must be intellectual, not purely economic.

The right reasons: The core foundations for success

The motivations that actually sustain scholars through the entire process are always intrinsic. They are rooted in a deep, personal commitment to the work itself.

- **Insatiable intellectual curiosity:** You have a question that genuinely keeps you up at night, and you need to be the one to answer it. This passion for a specific topic, theory, or problem is the core engine of the entire endeavor.

- **A drive for mastery and deep skill:** You want to become the undisputed expert in a narrow field, mastering not just the knowledge, but the methodological tools required to advance that knowledge.

- **Genuine tolerance for ambiguity:** You recognize that research is fundamentally about working in the dark. You are comfortable with slow progress, repeated failure, and having to invent the path rather than follow a map.

- **Commitment to the research lifestyle:** You understand that a PhD is not an academic qualification; it is an apprenticeship into the lifestyle of an independent researcher. You are committed to the autonomy, discipline, and scholarly contribution this lifestyle demands.

So, wouldn't it be handy if there was a thorough checklist of sorts to help PhD scholars think deep and hard before signing up for the PhD? Wait! Before moving on to the PhD introspection checklist, you must decide on the best entry route for you.

The preparation pathway: Master's vs. direct entry

A common point of confusion is whether to pursue a Master's degree before applying for a PhD (the "traditional" route) or to apply directly after a Bachelor's (the "direct entry" or integrated route, common in the US/Canada). The right answer depends entirely on your background, your field, and your confidence.

The Master's first advantage (Traditional route)

Taking a Master's degree is almost always recommended if you:

- Need topic clarity: You know your general field (e.g., neuroscience) but not your specific research question (e.g., neural mechanisms of decision fatigue). A Master's project provides two years to define your focus.

- Need experience: You lack high-level, independent research experience, publications, or conference presentations. The Master's is a low-stakes training ground.

- Need funding leverage: A Master's degree with a strong dissertation and publication record makes you a far more competitive applicant for PhD funding and top-tier programs.

- Need a safety net: If you realize academia isn't for you, you walk away with an advanced degree that has significant market value.

The direct entry advantage (Integrated route)

Applying directly from a Bachelor's degree is viable if you:

- Have exceptional clarity: You already have a Master's-level research focus and a powerful academic mentor from your undergraduate studies who can attest to your research maturity.

- Have extensive research background: You have already accumulated significant research hours (e.g., five years of lab experience, multiple first-author publications, substantial technical skill) that exceed the typical Master's output.

- Are confident in your choice: You are absolutely certain you want the full doctoral training and are comfortable with the longer time commitment (often 5-7 years) that direct entry entails, which includes the Master's-level coursework.

In short: A Master's is the safest way to prepare and demonstrate readiness; direct entry is only for those who are already operating at a Master's level when they finish their Bachelor's degree. So, don't make the mistake of evaluating your entry based on the numbers of years saved by skipping a step as it will cost you a whole lot more down the line if you opt for the wrong entry point.

With your intrinsic motivation clarified and your optimal preparation pathway selected, it is time to move from general concepts to personal accountability. The following checklist is designed to formalize your self-audit, confirming that your mindset is equipped to handle the specific realities of the PhD process.

Your personal PhD introspection checklist

Use the following questions to challenge your assumptions and confirm your commitment. Answer honestly—your future depends on it and your future is your own to build.

1. The commitment check (Motivation & drive)

- **The topic:** If you were not being paid, would you still spend 10 hours a week reading and thinking about your research topic?

- **The failure:** If your first two major experiments or data collection efforts fail completely, will you feel motivated to redesign and start over, or will you feel defeated and quit?

- **The isolation:** Can you handle working alone, managing your own schedule, and being the primary source of your daily accountability and progress for long stretches of time?

- **The opportunity cost:** What salary and professional momentum are you willing to sacrifice right now for the chance to pursue this question?

2. *The skillset and tolerance check (Personality & process)*

- **The process over product:** Do you enjoy the act of defining a problem, meticulously planning a method, and debating the nuances of theory more than you enjoy receiving a final answer or grade?

- **The feedback loop:** When a draft of your work is returned with brutal, heavily critical feedback, is your primary reaction: (A) Anger/Defense, or (B) Acknowledgment that this is a necessary step for improvement?

- **The administrative burden:** Are you prepared for the significant non-research work—teaching, administration, grant writing, and bureaucratic compliance—that consumes up to 50% of a researcher's life?

3. *The career and financial check (The launchpad)*

- **The post-PhD role:** When you envision your ideal job five years after earning the PhD, is that role inaccessible without the doctorate? If a Master's degree or industry certification could get you there, reconsider the PhD.

- **The non-academic path:** Are you willing to embrace career paths outside of traditional tenure-track academia (e.g., industry R&D, government policy, data science) as a valid and desirable outcome of your training?

- **The financial reality:** Have you realistically budgeted for the stipend level in your chosen geography and factored in the cost of living and the potential delay in high-income earnings?

If your honest answers confirm that your motivation is intrinsic, your mindset is durable, and your chosen career path genuinely requires the degree, you have completed the single most important step. You are ready to move from introspection to action.

Now that your commitment is confirmed, the next challenge is transforming that commitment into a strategic plan for entry. The first tactical decision you will make is *where* you will undertake this journey. Let's address this next.

2

Strategic university selection (Home vs abroad)

After establishing your **intrinsic motivation** and commitment (Chapter 1), the tactical decision-making process begins. The first and most critical choice is defining the geographical and institutional context for your work: *where* you will pursue your PhD.

The choice of university is often driven by prestige or a superficial desire for novelty. In reality, the strategic choice is about optimizing three factors: **Supervisor Fit, Research Infrastructure, and Career Trajectory.**

The false dichotomy: Home vs. abroad

The decision to pursue a PhD domestically or internationally is often framed as a choice between comfort and glamour. For the scholar's compass to remain oriented, this must be an unbiased, calculated decision based on research alignment, not perceived lifestyle.

Debunking the myths of studying abroad

The "Study Abroad" path is frequently romanticized. Scholars often chase an idealized, global experience that masks the harsh realities of doctoral research in a foreign context.

- **Myth of superiority vs. reality of output:** The myth suggests studying abroad automatically guarantees a superior education or global job prospects. **The reality is** the quality of a PhD is defined almost entirely by your **supervisor, your project, and your output** (publications). A world-class supervisor at home trumps an average one abroad.

- **Myth of glamorous stipends vs. reality of CoL:** The myth promises a foreign stipend that funds a glamorous lifestyle of travel and exploration. **The reality is** stipends are tightly calculated for local cost-of-living (CoL). You will likely spend your time budgeting, struggling with bureaucracy, and working long hours, just as you would at home. The sense of isolation in a new culture can be intense.

- **Myth of easy immigration vs. reality of visa pressure:** The myth is that it's easier to stay in the foreign country after graduation. **The reality is** post-PhD visa and immigration systems are complex, demanding, and often require immediate employment, creating immense pressure during the final dissertation writing phase.

- **Myth of a fresh start vs. reality of social capital:**

The myth implies a foreign start is a clean slate, free from all previous academic baggage. **The reality is** your academic reputation, publications, and network follow you. You start from zero social capital in a new country, which adds a heavy mental load to an already difficult process.

Unbiased evaluation: When to choose which path

The right choice is the one that minimizes friction and maximizes research output.

Choose your home country when:

- **National network is key:** Your research requires access to local infrastructure, specialized national data sets, or clinical/industry contacts only available at home.

- **Cultural context matters:** Your research is intrinsically linked to local policy, history, or culture that demands nuanced fluency and native perspective.

- **Time and cost are constrained:** You have family or financial commitments that make relocation and establishing a new life (visas, housing, banking, language barriers) an unacceptable burden.

- **Supervisor is perfect fit:** The undisputed global leader in your hyper-specific sub-field is already at your home institution.

Choose abroad when:

- **Methodological gap:** The specific methodological expertise, unique equipment, or theoretical approach essential for your project simply does not exist at a comparable level in your home country.

- **Career pivot:** You are intentionally using the PhD to pivot your long-term career to that specific international market (e.g., relocating for a specific global industry hub).

- **Irreplaceable mentor:** The only supervisor in the world who can meaningfully guide your project is based abroad, and no comparable local alternative exists.

Regardless of whether you choose to stay in your home country or venture abroad, the decision now funnels down to micro-level alignment, *i.e.,* your non-negotiables.

Strategic evaluation framework: 3 non-negotiables

Every PhD application must be built around the following three core non-negotiables, as they determine your daily reality and long-term success.

1. Supervisor fit (The most important variable)

The single greatest predictor of PhD success is the relationship with your supervisor. Prestige is temporary; conflict with your mentor is permanent.

- **Alignment:** Is their current research active and are they publishing in your **exact** sub-area, or are they pivoting?

Do not accept a supervisor who says, "Your project sounds interesting, let's try it" unless you are able to take full onus and lead the project yourself.

- **Track record:** How many students have they successfully graduated in the last five years? What are their graduates doing now? (Avoid "graveyards"—labs where students linger but never finish).

- **Mentorship style:** Are they hands-on, hands-off, or somewhere in between? This must align with your personality (e.g., do you need weekly check-ins or only semi-annual meetings?).

2. Research infrastructure and resources

Your environment must be a force multiplier for your research, not a limiting factor.

- **The ecosystem:** Does the university offer complementary strengths (e.g., if you are in Electrical Engineering, does the adjacent Psychology department provide the user studies infrastructure you need)?

- **Funding transparency:** Is the stipend guaranteed for the full duration of the PhD (e.g., 4 years)? What are the specific teaching and grant requirements attached to your funding?

- **Peer group:** Will you be surrounded by high-performing peers who challenge your thinking, or are you joining an isolated group? Peer support is a critical, often overlooked, resource.

3. Career and life trajectory

View the university as a launchpad, not a destination.

- **Post-Doc/job placement:** Where do the department's graduates land? Ask specific questions about placement rates in the sectors you care about (academia vs. industry).
- **Institution's reputation in the field:** A university's overall brand name (e.g., "Ivy League") matters less than its *specific* departmental reputation in your niche.
- **Life feasibility:** Beyond the lab, can you thrive there? Consider proximity to family, climate, and the general cultural fit. Burnout is minimized when the non-academic aspects of your life are stable.

Your strategic choice is not about choosing the "best" university, but the **best *fit*** for the unique demands of your project and your personality. Once you have the best fit university it's time to sort the next question in your PhD journey- *who* you are going to do your PhD with- i.e., your prospective Supervisor, the anchor mentor. Once you have a shortlist of well-fitting supervisors and institutions, the next step is to make contact.

3

The art of cold outreach to prospective PhD advisors

You have a meticulously curated shortlist of institutions and, critically, specific prospective advisors whose work aligns with your own (Chapter 2). The next step is not simply sending any arbitrary "Hello Prof" email; it is executing the first, high-stakes phase of your application: **strategic cold outreach**.

This process is not a generic mass mailing. It is a targeted research project where the subject is the prospective advisor, and the deliverable is their focused attention. The goal is simple: to prove that you are worth their time *before* you even submit a formal application. Remember, you are not the only one doing this and a Professor likely gets hundreds if not thousands of such cold emails on a daily basis filling up their inbox. So, you have to do your best to not get your email deleted or marked as spam right away.

The outreach mindset: Research, not request

Most cold emails fail because they treat the advisor as an admissions officer or, worse, adopt a desperate tone ("Do you have a PhD position?") that frames the interaction as a transaction. A successful cold email treats the advisor as a **collaborator**. They are busy; your email must respect their time and clearly demonstrate that you have done your homework hence, respecting your own time and efforts.

Here is how to prepare for the cold outreach:

Phase 1: Pre-contact research

Before you type the first word, you must identify your value proposition and the specific connection point.

- **Read their latest work:** Do not cite a paper from five years ago. Find their most recent publication (within the last 12-18 months) or a recent grant abstract. Reference this work specifically.
- **Pinpoint the gap:** Identify a specific gap, limitation, or future research direction mentioned in their recent paper that aligns with your interest area. This is your bridge to establish synergies.
- **Check for current availability:** Look at their lab website, social media, or institutional profile. Do they explicitly state they are *not* taking students? If so, respect that, or you will immediately be marked as someone who

doesn't follow instructions.

- **Know the admission cycle:** Understand the specific application windows, departmental deadlines, and typical funding decision timelines. This ensures your outreach is timed when the advisor is actively reviewing applications, maximizing the chance they will engage with your pitch.

- **Know the funding cycle:** Understand if their research is funded by a large, active grant. Mentioning an alignment with a specific grant they currently hold (e.g., "I saw your NSF grant on X, and my background in Y would be highly applicable to phase three...") shows strategic insight.

The optimal timing for cold outreach

Timing is a hidden factor in cold outreach success. Hitting an advisor's inbox when they are stressed or overwhelmed guarantees your email will be deleted or, ignored.

When to start (The golden window): Begin your initial outreach **4 to 6 weeks before the official departmental application deadline.** This window gives the advisor enough time to reply, request your documents, and encourage you to apply, but it is not so early that they forget you by the time official review begins. **Avoid sending emails** during major university breaks (winter holidays, summer vacation) or during peak grading weeks (end of term). What would be even better is if you can time your outreach to an upcoming major conference ask for a brief in-person meeting. A face-to-face meeting is always more impactful than a cold outreach and helps build a rapport.

When to stop (The cut-off): Stop all cold outreach to a specific institution **the moment you submit your formal application.** Once your application is submitted, the process moves to the admissions committee. Continuing to email the advisor after this point shows a lack of trust in the system and risks making you appear impatient or difficult to work with. Let the formal process take its course.

Phase 2: Crafting the perfect cold outreach pitch

A successful cold email is brief, targeted, and structured to be read in under 60 seconds.

1. The subject line: The Hook

The subject line must contain your intent, your name, and the specific link to their work. Avoid vague titles like "PhD Inquiry" or "Research Interest."

Weak Example: PhD Inquiry

Strong Example: Prospective PhD - Alignment with [Specific Paper Title] / [Your Name]

Best Example: Application to [Specific Lab Name] - Proposed Extension of [Advisor's Recent Finding]

2. The body: The three paragraph rule

Keep the body text concise and structured into three distinct paragraphs.

Paragraph 1 (The Hook & Connection): State your name, current affiliation, and explicitly mention the piece of their work you read and how it resonated with your background. *Example:* "I am [Your Name], a recent graduate of [University] with experience in [Specific Skill/Method]. I recently read your 2024 paper on [Topic], and I was particularly interested in your discussion of [Specific Limitation/Gap]."

Paragraph 2 (The Pitch & Value): Articulate the specific research question you would pursue *under their guidance* that addresses the gap you identified. This proves you have a project ready to go. Then, summarize your key skill set (e.g., Python, advanced statistics, field experience) that makes you the best person for this job. *Example:* "Building on this work, my proposal is to investigate [Specific Research Idea]. My previous experience developing [Specific Code/Model] aligns perfectly with the data analysis component mentioned in your future directions."

Paragraph 3 (The Ask & Logistics): Conclude with a low-friction request. Do not ask for an hour-long meeting. Ask for 15 minutes to discuss your proposed project or for confirmation of their student-taking status. *Example:* "I would be grateful for the opportunity to have a brief 10-15 minute video call to discuss this proposed direction further, or, if time is constrained, to simply confirm if you are considering new students for the Fall 20XX intake."

3. Attachments & links: The supporting evidence

Do not attach any unsolicited documents (CV, Transcript, Proposal) despite this being the most popular advice on the internet. And, here is why none of my mentees sends attachments right away. An email with an attachment is often the first to be discarded due to file security and storage concerns.

The wait strategy: If the advisor is interested, they will invariably reply with, "Please send me your CV and transcript." This request is a crucial **foot in the door**—it confirms their interest and ensures your documents are viewed when they are ready for them. Follow their lead precisely.

Phase 3: The follow-up protocol

If you receive no response after the initial email, do not despair. Busy academics often have overflowing inboxes. This is where the **series of sprints** approach to the PhD begins.

- **Wait protocol:** Wait at least **10-14 days** before sending a polite, professional follow-up.
- **Content:** Keep the follow-up email short. Simply resend the original email thread with a new, very brief message in the body:

"Dear Professor [Name],

Just following up on the email below regarding my interest in your lab.

Please let me know if you are currently considering new doctoral students.

Thank you for your time."

- **The final step:** If you receive no response after the second email, move on. Your time is finite, and a lack of response often signals a lack of availability (or poor organizational habits), neither of which are conducive to a successful supervisory relationship. Spamming a Faculty member with multiple follow ups and chasing them for a response doesn't better your odds. So, move on and invest your time with other shortlisted Advisors.

Your ability to manage the cold outreach process—to conduct the research, draft the compelling pitch, and manage the logistics—is the first demonstration of the professional rigor required for your PhD. But you are just getting started.

Securing an initial conversation is only half the battle; the next, more crucial test is to evaluate whether the potential advisor's style, expectations, and support system truly align with your needs. You must now move from demonstrating value to assessing compatibility.

4

Vetting your future supervisor (Pre-acceptance)

You have succeeded in the cold outreach sprint: you demonstrated your value, secured an interview, and have the first tentative foot in the door. Now, the roles reverse. You are no longer the applicant begging for a position; you are a highly-qualified candidate performing **due diligence** on your future supervisor.

Committing to a PhD is not just committing to a research question; it is committing to a **multi-year professional partnership**. The quality of this relationship is the single greatest predictor of doctoral success and well-being. This chapter outlines the three critical pillars you must evaluate *before* you say yes.

The three pillars of fit

The advisor-advisee relationship must be assessed across three dimensions. A perfect score on one does not compensate for a failing grade on another.

Intellectual fit: Alignment of research philosophy

This goes beyond simply liking their papers. It assesses whether your research direction can be successfully nurtured in their lab and whether they possess the specific expertise you need.

Managerial fit: Working style and expectations

This is the most overlooked pillar. An advisor is primarily your boss and mentor. You must understand their management style, their work ethic, and their logistical expectations for your time and output. A mismatch here leads to daily friction that can easily become unmanagable.

Cultural fit: Lab environment and support

This assesses the human element: the health of the lab culture, the availability of funding, and the presence of a strong network. You are joining a professional family; its atmosphere will dictate your daily mental health.

The interview strategy: Your questions

The interview is your chance to gather non-negotiable information. Do not use this time to re-pitch your CV; use it to ask questions that reveal the truth about the three pillars.

Questions for intellectual fit

1. How has your research agenda shifted in the last two years, and where do you see the next major area of focus for your lab? (This tests their current direction.)
2. In what specific area do you see my Masterful Research Question (or proposal) fitting into your current work and existing grants? (This tests active alignment.)
3. How do you typically handle students whose research evolves significantly away from the initial proposal? (This tests flexibility.)

Questions for managerial fit

1. What are your core expectations for communication frequency—weekly meetings, monthly check-ins, or only when necessary? (This sets the communication rhythm.)
2. What are your expectations regarding working hours, particularly for graduate students? (This tests work-life boundaries.)
3. What is your philosophy on student authorship? In what scenarios is a student typically the first author

versus a middle author? (This tests professional reward structure.)

4. What is your funding approach for the full duration of the PhD, including summer months and travel to international conferences? (This tests financial security.)

Questions for cultural fit

1. What are the key responsibilities—teaching, fieldwork, or grant writing—that students in your lab typically handle? (This tests labor expectations.)
2. What is the typical timeline for students to pass their candidacy/qualifying exams in your lab? (This tests project management success.)
3. How do you manage disagreements or conflicts that arise between you and your students, or between students within the lab? (This tests conflict resolution style.)

There is one other invaluable source of information that you should definitely tap into- the current and past lab members.

The unofficial audit: Talking to students of the lab/group

The most accurate data on an advisor is always held by their current and former students. Always insist on speaking with at least one current student *privately,* without the advisor present. This is a non-negotiable step.

When speaking to them (including alumni), focus on asking process-oriented questions rather than opinion-based ones.

1. What is the average response time for a draft you submit? (Process question that reveals their speed and dedication to feedback.)
2. Describe a time when you had a research setback or failure. How did the Professor respond? (Process question that reveals their support style under pressure.)
3. How often do you meet with the Professor, and is the meeting typically initiated by you or by them? (Process question that reveals the balance of control.)
4. How often do people in the lab collaborate, and what is the general social atmosphere like? (Process question that reveals the lab culture.)
5. Have any students left the lab prematurely, and what was the reason? (Direct question to uncover serious red flags.)
6. What is the most common career trajectory of the past lab members? Did they join industry or become faculty? (Helps you evaluate post graduation prospects and support)

Note: If the prospective advisor refuses to let you speak privately with their current students, consider this a major red flag and proceed with extreme caution. Transparency is key to trust.

Evaluating fit is a cold calculation, not an emotional decision. If you find a strong alignment across all three pillars, you are ready to make a commitment. If you find multiple areas of misalignment, be prepared to walk away—a bad fit is more costly than no PhD at all. Your commitment is professional, but the journey itself is intensely personal.

Now that you have committed to the right person in the right place, it is time to dismantle the idealized version of this journey. The next chapter strips away the glamor and prepares you for the operational reality of doctoral life.

5

The PhD myth vs. reality

The biggest hurdle in your PhD is often not the research itself, but the gulf between the journey you *expected* and the one you are *living, i.e.,* mismatched expectations. We are socially conditioned to believe that advanced study is a straightforward, intellectually pure pursuit. The reality is that it is a complex, emotionally taxing, and highly bureaucratic initiation that doesn't come with a preset instruction manual.

To successfully navigate this journey, you must first dismantle the comforting, yet harmful, myths that pervade academia.

Myth 1: The Illusion of the straight line smooth sailing journey

REALITY: Progress is an iterative spiral. Your compass is your guide.

You imagine a steady, upward-sloping graph of progress, but the PhD is filled with necessary steps backward. You will spend months on a research path that fails, or you'll rewrite chapters you thought were finished. Not just you, I had to do this too and this is also how this book was born and published in its current form. This non-linearity is not a sign of your failure; it's a sign that you are doing high-level research.

The belief that you can follow a **static roadmap** is the first, most dangerous mistake you will make. A roadmap is a printed path based on a fixed plan; it cannot account for a faulty experiment, an uncooperative data set, a change in committee membership, or a global event. When the predetermined path fails—and it *will* fail—the brittle roadmap model leads to crippling **self-blame** and burnout.

Thus, this book offers a **compass** instead of a map. A compass gives you a *direction* (your research question) and teaches you to trust your internal calibration to navigate the terrain as it actually exists and ask the right questions. Embrace the spiral; the mandatory detours are where the most profound intellectual discoveries are made. **Trust your compass to guide you, not a faulty roadmap to contain you.**

Myth 2: The glamour of breakthroughs

REALITY: Discovery is the result of relentless, often boring, discipline.

The public image is one of "Eureka!" moments and elegant presentations. The daily reality is the lonely grind: staring at a blinking cursor, debugging code for a week, or spending a full weekend formatting two hundred references. Your life is not the TED talk; it is the meticulous, quiet work that makes the TED talk possible. Expect disciplined work, not constant genius.

Myth 3: The "Expert" status

REALITY: The PhD is a license to manage intellectual uncertainty.

You are not graduating with a certificate of comprehensive knowledge. The true mark of a master learner is the ability to ask the best questions, define the *limits* of current understanding, and be genuinely comfortable with the fact that no one—including you and your supervisor—have all the answers and that's OK.

Myth 4: The 9-to-5 Job

REALITY: The PhD is an entrepreneurial lifestyle.

There is no HR department, no set office hours, no paid leaves, and often no external structure forcing you to stop working. The work expands to fill the time available. This freedom demands that **Boundaries** become your only defense against chronic overwork. You must explicitly define your workday, your week, and your breaks- you are in charge now.

Myth 5: The perfect dissertation

REALITY: The dissertation is a proof of concept.

The dissertation is a well-defended demonstration of your research competency, not the definitive, flawless magnum opus of your career. The belief that it must be perfect leads directly to **Analysis Paralysis** and prevents submission. Done is always better than perfect. The same applies to the research manuscripts you'll write over the course of your PhD.

Myth 6: The supportive Boss

REALITY: Your Supervisor is a professional stakeholder in *Your* project.

While they may be a great mentor, their primary role is professional: they control your funding, gatekeep your degree, and guide your career. You must treat this as a formal professional relationship, proactively **managing their expectations** and not passively waiting for their direction or therapeutic support. You are way past hand-holding stages if you've signed up for a PhD.

Myth 7: Financial security

REALITY: Financial precarity is the default for most PhDs.

Even with a solid scholarship, the struggle for competitive grants, RA-ships, and decent wages is a constant, non-academic stressor. You must plan for financial uncertainty and actively seek opportunities to supplement your income, as your academic work rarely covers your true cost of living.

Myth 8: The objective feedback

REALITY: Feedback is subjective, often contradictory, and must be filtered.

Your committee, peers, and reviewers will frequently disagree on the core argument, methods, or tone of your work. Your job is not to appease everyone, but to **synthesize** these competing views into a cohesive, evidenced defense of *your* own intellectual vision. You are the ultimate decision-maker.

Myth 9: The isolation of the genius

REALITY: You are an entrepreneur of knowledge.

While the research itself is solitary, career success—whether in or outside academia—depends entirely on your ability to **network**, collaborate, and proactively build a professional community. True intellectual breakthroughs rarely happen in a vacuum; they require constructive social friction.

Myth 10: Finish faster, be smarter

REALITY: Timeline is dictated by data, bureaucracy, and people.

Your time-to-degree is less a measure of your intellect and more a function of your experimental needs (e.g., long data collection cycles), institutional review board schedules, the responsiveness of your committee, and funding deadlines. These external forces are often beyond your immediate control.

Myth 11: Publish when it's ready

REALITY: Publish work-in-progress (WIP) to claim intellectual property early.

Waiting until a chapter or manuscript is "perfect" before sharing it risks being scooped and prevents you from building a public research profile. You must strategically release partial results (conference abstracts, working papers) to stake your claim and gain crucial early feedback. The research field moves quickly and no idea is so unique that only you'd be working on it at any given time.

Myth 12: Sacrifice for the degree

REALITY: The PhD works best when it supports a sustainable life.

Sacrificing your core relationships, health, and hobbies is not a mark of dedication; it is a recipe for chronic burnout and deep personal regret. The PhD is a ~~marathon~~, ~~sprint~~, series of sprints, and your stamina depends entirely on protecting your time for rest and non-academic fulfillment.

Myth 13: Mental health is a personal failure

REALITY: Mental strain is an occupational hazard.

The high stakes, intense isolation, power dynamics, and financial stress inherent in academia make psychological support (therapy, counseling, mindfulness) a mandatory resource, not a sign of personal weakness. Seek help immediately and without shame.

Myth 14: The global academic rule book (For Study Abroad/International Scholars)

REALITY: Your visa and cultural alignment dictate research decisions.

For international scholars, the challenge is multiplied: you are navigating the foreign national culture *and* a new academic culture simultaneously. Furthermore, your **visa status** and funding body's mandates often create non-negotiable constraints on your PhD journey that local students often do not face. These administrative pressures must be factored into your research plan.

Myth 15: The Dissertation is your legacy

REALITY: Your transferable skills are the true lasting currency and your dissertation doesn't define you.

The final document is important, but its influence is often confined to a niche. Your true legacy and most valuable asset are the **transferable skills** you gained: expert project management, complex data analysis, cross-cultural communication, persuasive grant writing, and rigorous critical thinking. These skills are what launch your successful career, whether you pursue a tenure-track position or a role in industry.

The unspoken context: Why these myths persist

These illusions persist because they serve the institutional culture—they romanticize the work, promote endless dedication, and obscure the systemic issues that cause scholar distress. Your commitment to **reality** is your first act of self-care and professional maturity.

Now that we have confronted these pervasive myths of a typical PhD journey, let's talk about burnout, explore its symptoms and the structures you need to build to successfully navigate the terrain.

6

Internal burnout calibration

You can have the most strategic plan and the most supportive supervisor, but if your internal operating system fails, the PhD invariably fails. The academic environment is a pressure cooker designed for high performers, and while it promises rigor, it frequently delivers **burnout**. This exhaustion is rarely a sudden crash; it is the slow, implicit erosion of passion, energy, and cognitive ability. This chapter moves beyond recognizing the problem to building the internal structures and daily calibration required to survive and thrive.

More than just stress: Symptoms of academic exhaustion

Stress is a natural part of a PhD (somewhat normal up to a certain extent), but burnout is a different beast entirely and shouldn't be taken lightly. Stress can be a motivator, pushing you to meet a deadline. Burnout is a state of emotional, physical, and mental exhaustion caused by prolonged, excessive stress. It's when your fuel tank is completely empty and the stress has become chronic. The key signs of burnout are:

- a feeling of constant fatigue that sleep doesn't fix,
- a cynical and detached attitude toward your work and colleagues,
- a feeling of ineffectiveness, and
- a profound loss of the joy you once had for your research.

It's crucial to distinguish between a bad week and a serious pattern. If you've felt this way for an extended period—months, not days—you may be experiencing burnout. Acknowledging these symptoms is the first and most critical step to addressing them. You cannot fix a problem you refuse to see. Give yourself permission to recognize that something is wrong so you can start to make it right before it gets out of control.

The academic pressure cooker: Identifying root causes in your environment

Burnout doesn't appear overnight. It's often fueled by a mix of factors unique to the academic environment. These can include unclear expectations from your supervisor, a sense of isolation from working alone for long hours, the constant pressure to publish or perish, and a relentless focus on output over well-being. The competitive nature of academia, combined with the lack of clear, structured milestones, can create a perfect storm for emotional and mental exhaustion.

This chapter will help you identify the specific pressures in your own environment. These academic pressures may look something like:

- Is your supervisor's feedback too vague?
- Are you comparing yourself too much to a peer who seems to have it all together?
- Are you feeling unsure if you are doing too much or too little?
- Is your goal post being moved too frequently for you to progress?
- Struggling to live off your stipend always look for the next paycheck?
- Are you experiencing intense isolation from long, solitary work hours?
- Do you feel lack of a support system as the only one working on a niche topic?
- …………………….. and more

Pinpointing the sources of your stress is the key to creating targeted strategies to manage them. You can't solve a problem until you understand its root cause.

A self-assessment: Where are you on the burnout spectrum?

To move forward, you need to know where you stand. Below is a simple introspection exercise to help you gauge your current level of burnout. Be honest with yourself. This isn't about judgment; it's about awareness.

Rate yourself on a scale of 1 (never) to 5 (always) for each statement:

1. I feel emotionally drained and exhausted at the end of the day.
2. I am cynical about my work and my field.
3. I feel detached or distant from my research.
4. I feel ineffective and unable to accomplish anything worthwhile.
5. I dread starting my workday.
6. I often feel overwhelmed by the amount of work I have to do.
7. I have a hard time sleeping or staying asleep.
8. I have noticed a decline in my physical health (e.g., frequent headaches, stomach issues).
9. My concentration level has significantly dropped, making reading or writing feel like a struggle.
10. I consistently procrastinate on important, high-priority

tasks (like writing a core chapter or running data analysis).
11. I get easily irritated or defensive when receiving feedback from my supervisor or peers.
12. I feel obligated, rather than motivated, to work on my research.
13. I frequently forget key information or feel my memory is failing me when discussing my research.
14. I have significantly reduced my social activities or hobbies to focus (unproductively) on work.
15. Even when I take a break, I feel guilty or worried about my unfinished work.
16. I find myself making basic, careless mistakes in my experiments, citations, or writing.
17. I actively avoid communication or meetings with my supervisor or committee members.
18. I feel like I have to put in an excessive amount of effort just to achieve mediocre results.
19. I frequently feel resentment towards my peers or supervisor, even when they are trying to help.
20. I have started relying more heavily on caffeine, alcohol, or other substances to cope with work demands.

Scoring:

- **< 30:** You are likely experiencing normal PhD stress. Focus on prevention and building good habits.
- **30-60:** You are at risk of burnout. It's time to take proactive steps to address your stress levels.
- **> 60:** You are likely experiencing burnout. It's crucial

to seek help, whether from a professional therapist, a trusted mentor, or a university support service. This is your wake-up call to change course.

Understanding where you land on this spectrum is powerful. If your score indicates a *moderate to high risk* of burnout, it's not a failure; it's a clear call to action. The next step in trusting your compass is re-calibrating your direction by reconnecting with the core motivation that brought you here—your "Why"—which is exactly what we'll dive into next.

7

Reconnecting with your "why"

The daily grind can make you forget the reason you embarked on this journey in the first place. You started a PhD because a problem fascinated you. A question kept you up at night. However, the minutiae of data collection, writing, revision and setbacks can obscure that initial passion. To fight burnout, you must intentionally reconnect with that original spark.

Take a moment to think back to the person you were when you started.

What was the core fascination?

What problem were you so excited to solve?

It's time to recapture your "why".

Tool: The "why" post-it

Write your core fascination or the problem that drives you on a Post-it note. Put it next to your computer. Look at it when you're feeling bogged down. Your "why" is your most powerful fuel. When the external motivation from deadlines or a supervisor's encouragement wanes, your intrinsic passion is what will keep you going.

Values alignment: Ensuring your work resonates with your core beliefs

A PhD is a long commitment, and it's easy to get lost in the details of a project that no longer feels meaningful. We'll explore how to ensure your project still aligns with your personal values and what you believe is important.

Do you value social justice, environmental sustainability, or perhaps pure intellectual discovery? Your work should, on some level, connect to these values.

If you find that your project has drifted away from your core values, it's not too late to course-correct. This might mean reframing your research question, changing your methodology, or even considering a new topic in consultation with your supervisor. When your work and values are aligned, your motivation becomes unbreakable, because you're not just working on a project; you're working on something that matters to you personally.

The grand purpose: Connecting your niche research to the bigger picture

It's easy for your dissertation to feel like a tiny island in a vast ocean of knowledge. But that island is, in fact, connected to the mainland. Your niche research, no matter how specific, contributes to a broader conversation in your field and in the world. Seeing how your work fits into a grand purpose can re-energize your efforts and remind you of the value you're creating.

For example, a historian studying a small, forgotten event is helping us understand broader societal trends. A biochemist studying a single protein is contributing to our understanding of a major disease. A roboticist studying natural selection and evolution is helping us break barriers in design and technology and propose new bio-inspired design and traversal mechanisms for robots.

To ensure you can connect your specific, niche research to these broader conversations, we'll use the **Grand Purpose Connector** exercise below. This exercise forces you to translate your technical findings into statements that matter to the world outside your niche.

Exercise: The Grand Purpose Connector (The "So What?" framework)

Take your core research question and complete the three following statements:

1. **The niche:** My research specifically analyzes... (Focus on the highly technical, specific data/subject).
2. **The field:** My research contributes to my academic field by... (Focus on filling a gap in the existing literature).
3. **The grand purpose:** My research matters to the world because it changes/improves... (Focus on societal, policy, human, or intellectual impact).

This exercise helps you articulate the "so what?" of your work.
Who benefits from your research?
How does it change the way we think about a problem?

Answering these questions can give your work a renewed sense of purpose and meaning. Now that you can articulate the macro-level impact of your work (The Grand Purpose), the next challenge is to bring that sense of meaning down to the micro-level—your daily to-do list. An inspiring mission is useless if it doesn't inform what you do during work hours. This is where we move from 'Why' to 'How.'

The daily alignment: Translating your 'Why' into sustainable action plan

The core burnout symptom of feeling **ineffective**, **overwhelmed**, and struggling with **procrastination** as discussed in previous Chapter often stems from a disconnect between your grand purpose and your daily to-do list. A mission statement isn't enough; you need an operating manual. Your "Why" must be actively broken down into small, meaningful, and measurable tasks.

Instead of writing "Work on dissertation" (an overwhelming task), write "Write 500 words on the transition sentence of the introduction" or "Analyze 3 hours of data." This translates the abstract purpose into manageable quantifiable steps, transforming the feeling of being ineffective into daily **wins**. Small, consistent wins are the antidote to the burnout symptom of Reduced Personal Accomplishment. When you align your daily task to your core value, even monotonous work becomes purposeful.

But, there is one more consideration to be made for this daily alignment to work- the pacing. You need a sustainable pace to execute this task list over a sustained period of time and this is what we shall look into next.

The compassionate pacing: Embracing rest and imperfection

Many burnout signs are rooted in a culture of self-sacrifice and perfectionism. Your compass is a tool for *direction,* not relentless acceleration. It's vital to see rest not as a reward for work, but as a **mandatory input** for high-quality, sustainable research. When you are constantly **drained** or **forgetting information**, you are physically unable to perform high-level cognitive work.

True dedication is honoring your physical needs (like **sleep and health**) by setting hard boundaries. Furthermore, accepting that your work, especially early drafts, will be **imperfect** is crucial. The goal is progress, not instant perfection.

Self-compassion allows you to tolerate mistakes and recover quickly, which is essential for a journey as long as the PhD. This internal work—reconnecting with your "Why" and practicing self-compassion—is your strongest shield. However, that shield is fragile if you don't understand the forces attacking it. The feelings of **detachment**, **dread**, **irritation**, and **resentment** that you may have flagged are not solely products of internal failure. They are often a direct, logical response to the **ambiguity and hidden power structures** of academic culture. To truly protect your progress and peace of mind, you must move from *diagnosing the symptoms* to *decoding the source* of the pressure which will now look into.

You have now established your **unbreakable core**—your intrinsic motivation, your aligned values, and your commitment to compassionate, sustainable work. This internal foundation is essential, but it exists within a system that can be confusing and often hostile to well-being. The next step in building your armor is understanding the battlefield itself. In Chapter 8, we step outside the self to shine a light on the **unwritten rules, ambiguity, and hidden power dynamics of academic culture** that directly fuel burnout. Decoding these unspoken pressures is the final step in protecting your passion and peace of mind.

8

Decoding the unwritten rules of academic culture

Thus far, you've completed the crucial internal work: you've **oriented your compass** to ensure you are doing the PhD for the right reasons, vetted your **future supervisor's alignment, demystified** the PhD journey, diagnosed your specific **burnout symptoms**, and anchored your purpose to build the essential **shield of self-compassion**. This helps you address the internal causes of burnout. Now, we will look into the unwritten rules of academic culture- the rules that result in external forces that affect your PhD journey in one way or another.

Academia operates via a set of unwritten rules—rules about power, credit, and conduct that are never formally taught but are ruthlessly enforced. This chapter arms you with the knowledge to **decode these hidden dynamics**, directly tackling the root causes of your exhaustion by transforming systemic ambiguity into clear professional strategy.

Power dynamics and hierarchy: Navigating the advisor-advisee relationship

Your supervisor is not just a mentor; they are the ultimate **gatekeeper** of your PhD journey. The inherent power dynamic exists because your supervisor holds disproportionate control over the levers of your success: **funding and resources, the approval of your degree milestones (like confirmation of candidature), and your future career network (recommendation letters).**

Acknowledging that this relationship is hierarchical is the first step toward managing it. Understanding these power dynamics is crucial for navigating the relationship successfully. We'll teach you how to set clear boundaries, manage expectations, and communicate effectively, even when it feels intimidating. This is a partnership, and while the roles are different, you have a critical role to play in making it a successful one.

One key strategy is proactive communication. Instead of waiting for your supervisor to reach out, you should become a **proactive communicator**. This could mean that you schedule regular meetings and come prepared with a clear agenda. Ask for specific feedback on a single chapter, rather than a whole draft. By taking control of the communication, you can build a more productive and less stressful relationship.

The escalation ladder: When to bypass your supervisor

The unspoken rule is that you must handle all issues through your primary supervisor first. However, there are rare, critical times when your path is blocked, the relationship becomes toxic, or the issue is non-academic (e.g., funding discrepancy, harassment, discrimination).

You have the right to self-preservation. When an issue threatens your health, safety, or academic standing, or when repeated, documented attempts to resolve a serious issue with your supervisor have failed, you must escalate.

The Strategy (The ladder): Do not jump straight to the highest authority. Follow the academic escalation ladder:

1. **The Co-supervisor or committee member:** They are often aware of the dynamics and can mediate informally.
2. **The Department Head/Chair:** For conflicts, resources, or academic trajectory issues.
3. **The Graduate Program Director (GPD):** They are responsible for the administrative process and student well-being within the program.
4. **The Dean of the graduate school:** This is the final internal step for major appeals, formal complaints, or serious ethical breaches.

Crucial caveat: This step is irreversible. Document every prior attempt to resolve the issue (emails, meeting notes, etc.) before taking action. Bypassing your supervisor is a decision you make for your long-term survival, not a tool for short-term conflict avoidance.

Furthermore, the challenges in academia are not purely relational; they are often cultural. If you are pursuing a PhD in a foreign country, the burden of decoding your supervisor is compounded by the hidden tax of decoding an entire university and society. This leads us to the next unwritten rule that affects international scholars.

The rule of lost context: The international scholar's hidden burden

Doing a PhD abroad adds a layer of complexity that is never discussed: you are constantly running a **"cultural operating system" translator** in your mind. **Every interaction costs more energy than it should, and your default state is "outsider."**

You are not just dealing with academic jargon; you are decoding social and institutional subtexts that locals absorb intuitively (e.g., how informal is too informal with a supervisor, how to interpret a vague institutional email, the unspoken rules of a grant application that are only clear to those who grew up in that country). This constant decoding causes **cognitive overload** and **isolation**, accelerating burnout.

Here is how to approach this- **build a context bridge.** Actively seek out **non-research mentors** (admin staff, non-academic friends, other international students 2-3 years ahead of you) whose primary job is to help you translate context, not content. Don't be afraid to ask basic questions about local culture or how the university *really* works. Your success depends on finding people who can tell you what is obvious to everyone else.

Navigating the cultural landscape is a defensive measure to protect your energy. Once your energy is protected, you must strategically invest it into the public-facing measures of success—the currency of academia. Your worth isn't just about your dissertation; it's about your ability to translate that work into measurable professional metrics and disseminating your findings.

The currency of academia: Understanding publications, conferences, and grants

Beyond your dissertation, there's a whole world of academic currency. We'll break down why publications, conference presentations, and grant applications are so crucial for your future career.

Publications are the gold standard for communicating your research and building your reputation. Conferences are for networking and getting feedback on your work-in-progress. Journals are for more mature research ideas that have been vetted by peers. Grants are for securing funding and demonstrating your ability to lead a research project with a much larger impact.

It's easy to feel overwhelmed by the pressure to "do everything". We'll give you a mental model for understanding this system so you can make strategic decisions. You don't have to do it all at once. Focus on the opportunities that align with your stage and goals. For example, in your first year, attending a conference might be more valuable than trying to win a grant. This strategic thinking will help you manage your time and energy more effectively. But, how do you optimize your time at a conference and build your professional network?

The 5/5/5 networking rule

Conferences are not just for presenting your own work; they are job interviews. Many PhDs struggle because they treat networking like speed dating. The unwritten rule is that **quality wins over quantity.** It is better to have five meaningful conversations than 50 superficial handshakes.

This is where the **5/5/5 networking strategy** is very powerful. Before a conference, identify **five** specific people you must meet (a future collaborator, a journal editor, a target department hiring manager). For each of them, prepare a meeting time of **five minutes** or less, and have a clear, concise **five-sentence pitch** (your elevator pitch) about your research and why you wanted to meet them. This respects their time, makes you memorable, and drastically reduces social anxiety.

Even when you succeed at generating currency—be it a presentation or a paper—a much deeper, internal conflict often arises: the struggle to truly believe you earned it. This is the persistent ghost of imposter syndrome.

The imposter syndrome: Owning your intellectual space

If you've ever felt like a fraud, you're not alone—it's a near-universal PhD experience. Imposter syndrome is the feeling that you don't belong and that at any moment you'll be "found out." It often stems from a combination of perfectionism, external validation, and the competitive nature of academia. The more you know, the more you realize you don't know, which can make you feel even more like a fraud.

Tool: The success journal

To manage imposter syndrome, we'll give you a powerful tool: the **Success Journal**. Every week, write down a few small wins. These don't have to be major accomplishments. They could be a difficult paper you finally understood, a meeting where you presented a good idea, or a kind email from a colleague. This practice trains your brain to focus on your accomplishments, not just your shortcomings. You have earned your place here.

This internal work—the fight against imposter syndrome—is crucial, but it must be matched by external professionalism. Once you internalize your value and own your intellectual contribution, you must be prepared to defend it in the formal academic marketplace. This is especially true when it comes to managing the often-contradictory advice you receive.

The feedback funnel (Navigating contradiction)

The biggest source of anxiety is receiving contradictory advice from your supervisor, co-supervisor, and committee members—one tells you to do A, another tells you to do B. **The unwritten rule is that you are the project manager, and the responsibility for synthesizing contradictory advice is yours alone.** You cannot blame the disagreement on your committee.

Use this 3-Step funnel strategy to resolve contradictions and assimilate feedback:

1. **Acknowledge and document:** Thank each person for the feedback and log the contradiction (e.g., *Dr. X suggested Method A, Dr. Y suggested Method B*).
2. **Conduct due diligence:** Go to the literature and decide which method/direction is theoretically or empirically stronger for your specific project.
3. **Assert and justify (Closing the loop):** Do *not* ask for permission. Instead, close the loop by stating your synthesized decision and the data that supports it. Say: "I chose to proceed with **Method A** because the foundational literature by Scholar Z suggests it is better suited for analyzing Time-Series Data (as Dr. X implied). I've adjusted the introduction to reflect this theoretical commitment."

The successful management of feedback immediately leads to the most common external hurdle: securing formal credit for your work.

The hidden cost of collaboration: Authorship and credit

One of the greatest sources of conflict and anxiety among early career researchers is the unspoken expectation around **authorship and credit**. The unwritten rule is: *Never assume credit; always clarify it.*

Academic credit isn't a prize for showing up; it's a formal acknowledgment of intellectual contribution. Most fields rely on the following criteria for authorship for a contributor to be listed as an author/co-author:

1. Substantial contributions to the **conception or design** of the work; or the **acquisition, analysis, or interpretation** of data for the work.
2. **Drafting the work** or revising it critically for important intellectual content.
3. **Final approval** of the version to be published.
4. Agreement to be **accountable** for all aspects of the work.

The first author is usually the one who did the most work (often the PhD scholar), and the last author is usually the senior leader (often the supervisor).

The mandatory credit conversation

Often hard and somewhat overlooked conversation amongst collaborators is the credit conversation. Before any collaborative project begins, you **must** initiate a **Credit Conversation**. Ask directly:

- "What criteria will we use to determine authorship on

this specific paper, and who will be the first author?"

- "If I do the data collection and analysis, and you refine the writing, how will we determine the order?"
- "Who gets assigned the corresponding author?"

Having this (hard) professional conversation at the beginning eliminates the passive-aggressive tension and conflict that arises at the end of the project. **Protect your intellectual property by making the rules explicit before the work starts.** But, what if, you and your peer made significant strides in leading the work? Shared contributions and intellectual rights? How does that work?

Equal author contribution: Use this designation sparingly

In many fields, particularly those with highly collaborative or interdisciplinary projects, two or more authors may genuinely share the primary intellectual contribution. In this case, the footnote **"These authors contributed equally"** is used, often marked by an asterisk or dagger next to the author names.

This designation should be used *only* when the first two authors (or more) have truly provided an equivalent intellectual and time investment into the project's conception, execution, and manuscript drafting. It effectively grants both individuals the career benefit of being the "first author" for metrics and CV purposes.

But, use this designation **sparingly and with caution**. Do not use it as a tool to avoid a difficult conversation about who truly led the project. When in doubt, a clear first author (who led the drafting and analysis) followed by a clear second author is almost always preferable to avoid diluting the impact of the primary contributor. It must be a consensus decision, documented and agreed upon by all parties *before* submission.

The Data sunset clause (Post-graduation ownership)

The unwritten rule is that your **supervisor owns the raw data collected under their funding, but you own the analysis and interpretation** that form your dissertation. This ownership is a major point of negotiation when you leave. Before you submit your dissertation, get a written agreement (an email confirming the details is sufficient) specifying:

1. **Data access:** Will you maintain access to a redacted version of the dataset for post-doc or future research?
2. **Future publications:** Can you publish future papers based on the *current analysis* without your supervisor initiating the work? (This is crucial for establishing your own independent research trajectory.)
3. **Data retention:** How long will the lab legally archive the raw data? This protects you if future employers ask for confirmation.

Credit isn't just about what ends up on the CV; it's also about what *doesn't*. The next major trap involves the uncredited, administrative tasks that drain your time without advancing your career.

Invisible labor: The service vs. CV dilemma- When to say No?

This is the hidden labor sinkhole that costs early-career researchers dozens of hours. PhD students are often asked or pressured to take on low-status, non-CV-building service roles (e.g., organizing a seminar, administrative ad-hoc tasks). This uncredited service often leads directly to resentment and time famine.

Evaluate all non-research tasks by their CV/Network value. If an activity takes up more than 10 hours a month and does not result in a strong line on your CV (publication, grant, formal role) or a significant, strategic relationship, it is a primary burnout risk.

Learn to use a polite but firm filter for these requests. Instead of saying "no," say: "That sounds like a vital initiative. Given my commitment to finalizing my dissertation chapter next month, I can commit to **one small, bounded task** but will need to decline the role of **the large, time-consuming role**."

Defending your time is one side of the coin; defending your intellectual efforts against external critique is the other. The most painful form of critique is the one every researcher must master: rejection.

The editorial reality: Rejection is a mandated process

The unspoken rule of publishing is that **rejection is the default state.** Most top-tier journals reject over 90% of submissions. Learning to manage the emotional fallout of rejection is just as important as mastering the critique itself.

Your worth is not measured by the acceptance rate; your success is measured by your resilience. Treat the review process as an iterative game where the goal is refinement, not instant gratification.

Tool: The 24-Hour rule for resilience

When you receive a rejection, impose the **24-Hour rule**. For the first 24 hours, allow yourself to feel frustrated—don't look at the reviewer comments. After 24 hours, the emotional period ends. You put your professional hat back on, open the comments, and immediately create an action plan for revision and re-submission. **This strict boundary prevents rejection from derailing your entire week.**

The 24x7 expectation: Managing digital boundaries

The PhD is an entrepreneurial lifestyle, and the availability of email and messaging apps creates a false sense that you must always be "on." This digital demand severely erodes the rest time needed to prevent chronic exhaustion.

Your PI's working hours are not your working hours. You are not expected to respond to non-critical emails after

6 PM or on weekends. The culture rewards availability, but the individual pays the price in mental exhaustion.

Use time blocking during your working hours to process all email, and keep the inbox closed the rest of the time. This b**atching strategy** protects your focus, minimizes context switching, and clearly communicates that your priority is deep, analytical work.

While you protect your personal time through boundaries, you must proactively manage the institutional time requirements. Bureaucracy moves slowly, and the failure to anticipate administrative timelines is a common cause of graduation delay.

The administrative labyrinth: Mastering the bureaucracy

The university administration—the Graduate School, the Registrar, the Ethics Committee (Internal Review Board (IRB))—is the single biggest, non-academic factor in your time-to-degree. The unwritten rule is that **bureaucracy operates on its own timeline, and that timeline is slow and should be accounted for.**

You can be a genius, but if you don't submit your ethics proposal (IRB) six months before you need to start data collection (especially when animals or human participants are involved), you will be delayed. If you miss the narrow window to submit your final dissertation, you will be delayed by a semester.

You must treat every administrative deadline, especially those related to ethics approvals and final submission, with a **Bureaucracy Buffer**. If the official deadline is March 1st, make your personal deadline February 1st.

- **Ethics/IRB:** Start the application process the day you finalize your proposal methodology, not the day you need to start data collection.
- **Dissertation submission:** Assume your final draft will require two rounds of administrative checks and three days of unexpected computer failures. Build that time in.

Mastering bureaucracy means being ruthlessly organized, reading every institutional handbook, and proactively managing these time sinks, which are often the true gatekeepers of your graduation date.

Having mastered the rules of engagement—understanding the system's power dynamics, securing your credit, and navigating its administrative timelines—you are now operating from a position of professional strength. This procedural control allows you to shift your focus from simply *following the rules* to effectively **asserting your intellectual authority** within them. The final and most advanced unwritten rule is the ability to respectfully, yet firmly, defend the research propositions that define your degree.

Defending your research with respect

There will be times when you need to stand firm on a decision about your research direction or methodology. This is not disobedience; it is your intellectual duty as the expert on your specific dissertation.

When you disagree, use data and confidence, not emotion. Don't say, "I feel like this is better." Say: "I hear your concern about methodology B, but in reading the literature from Scholar X and Scholar Y, I believe methodology A is necessary because it is the only way to capture the variability in the Specific Data Set." Your job is to present a strong, evidenced case for your intellectual choice, turning a potential conflict into a productive scholarly discussion.

Having understood the unwritten rules of the PhD journey, you now possess the necessary intellectual awareness, but awareness is not enough to survive the long, isolating haul of the PhD.

Before you fully engage the system you now understand, you must prepare the vessel. The transition from applicant to working scholar is a seismic psychological event that requires specific, deliberate preparation. The next chapter pivots our focus to the **internal launch**—the specific mental and physical preparations required to successfully navigate the crucial first six months of your journey and build the stamina needed for the road ahead.

9

The mental kick-off and launch preparation

You have successfully navigated the entire application process, secured your position, and decoded the unwritten rules. You now know the **rules of the road** as clear as day. But before you can successfully drive, you must check your own internal engine. The time between acceptance and the official start date—and the first six months thereafter—is often overlooked, yet it is where the foundation of your long-term success, or failure, is set.

The PhD is an intense psychological shift. You move from a highly structured student environment (exams, set classes, clear assignments) to an unstructured, self-directed research environment. The mental challenge is not the complexity of the research; it is the **sudden, radical lack of structure** and the pressure to perform without external deadlines.

This chapter provides the critical launch strategy, ensuring you step onto campus with a plan for your mind, your health, and your logistics.

The psychological launch: From student to scholar

The most common trap for new PhD students is arriving mentally exhausted from the application process and expecting the program structure to carry them. This is the moment when you must switch your mindset from **task completion** (passing exams) to **project management** (running your dissertation like a business).

The great rest: Take a true, dedicated break (at least 4-6 weeks) before you start. Do not read your advisor's entire bibliography. Recharge your social batteries and reconnect with non-academic hobbies. PhDs are won by stamina, not by a head start. Don't save this for the first 4-5 weeks after your start your PhD.

Pre-empt the isolation: Doctoral work is isolating. Before you start, build a deliberate social contract with your partner, family, or friends. Clearly define when you are working and when you are *off*, and defend that boundary fiercely.

Define your exit criteria: While starting, think about finishing. What does a successful PhD look like to you? Is it an academic job, an industry role, or simply the degree itself? Write down this criterion now, as it will be your anchor when motivation inevitably dips. You don't want to end up at the finish line absolutely clueless about the next steps.

The Year 1 sanity checklist

The first year is about survival, adaptation, and establishing good habits, not achieving global fame. Use this checklist to structure your first 12 months, prioritizing mental health and systemic setup over raw output.

Logistical and mental setup to establish a non-academic routine: Schedule regular physical activity, dedicated relaxation time, and a fixed bedtime. The most valuable output is consistent output, which requires consistent rest.

Identify your non-supervisor mentor: Find a senior PhD student (Year 3 or 4) or a friendly postdoc who can answer the "stupid questions" you can't ask your advisor or GPD (Graduate Program Director).
Find your work tribe: Locate 2-3 colleagues (in or out of your discipline) who can serve as an intellectual and emotional support group for venting, proofreading, and commiseration. Be mindful not to convert this into a gossip crew.

Academic and professional setup: Become proficient in your citation manager tools, reference management software, and any lab-specific analysis tools *before* you need them for a deadline.

Map the coursework: Do not treat coursework as hurdles to jump. Every course should be viewed as an opportunity to generate literature review content or refine a chapter idea for your dissertation. Map out the requirements number of credits and courses that are mandatory so you know when to sign up for them in your PhD journey.

Map the PhD graduation requirements: Often times, graduation for a PhD program comes with a preset mandate often set by the University, Department or your advisor. Make sure to enlist and study these clearly including the minimal number and type of publications required to defend your dissertation.

Set your dissertation filing system: Create a ruthless, hyper-organized digital filing system for every article, draft, and dataset from day one. Good organization now saves hundreds of hours of frustration later.

Write for non-evaluation: Spend 30 minutes every day writing non-graded material (a blog post, an informal summary of a paper, journal entries). This lowers the emotional barrier to writing when the pressure is on.

The systemic and mental groundwork laid by this checklist is essential for all scholars. However, if you are crossing borders, you have an additional, non-negotiable layer of logistical complexity to manage.

The global scholar: Launch checklist for moving abroad

Moving internationally adds a hidden layer of complexity—the **Hidden tax of cross-border logistics**. Failing to address these issues early can consume your research time and energy for months. Treat this list as your pre-departure administrative priority.

Pre-departure documentation: Do not wait for the final admission letter; start the visa application process and financial evidence gathering as soon as the initial offer is confirmed. Always have paper copies of all official documents, including your offer letter.

Financial setup and banking: Establish a temporary international fund transfer method for the first month. Research and pre-open a local bank account *before* arrival, if possible, as this is often required for stipend direct deposit.

Health and insurance: Understand the local healthcare system (public vs. private) and ensure you have comprehensive health insurance coverage (provided by the university or independently secured) for the first 90 days.

Post-arrival formalities: Within the first week, register with the local council or police station (a mandatory step in many countries for foreign residents) to legalize your presence. Understand if there are any other formalities to be done as these often come with stipulated time frames and missing a step can have serious consequences.

Master public transport: Spend the first week figuring out the local bus, subway, and train routes. Independence relies on efficient, low-stress movement.

Find your ethnic hub: Immediately seek out a community or student group for your native language or culture. This provides a crucial, low-effort emotional safe space to retreat to when cognitive load is high. Aside from this, you can also find a group of like-minded sports fanatics to keep you mentally and physically engaged.

Find budget-friendly housing: Prioritize housing that matches your living style and fits your budget. A stressful accommodation will tank your productivity at work as you want to be well rested and refreshed for your research.

The work of the PhD begins long before the first class or the first data point. You have successfully completed **Part I: Orienting Your Compass**, defining your motivation, securing your position, and decoding the rules of the academic world. You are now intellectually and logistically ready to begin. However, readiness is not the same as **resilience**. The PhD is a long-term psychological and physical grind that requires a robust support network to ensure you not only finish, but you finish well.

We must now pivot from **preparation** to **protection**. **Part II: The resilience core—Partnership and well-being** will focus on building the two most crucial external defenses: proactively **managing the supervisor relationship** and establishing the **personal boundaries** necessary for long-term mental health.

II

The resilience core- Partnership and well-being

The PhD demands resilience beyond research. This Part focuses on building your defense system against isolation and pressure. We cover essential human elements: strategically managing the ***supervisor partnership****, cultivating a robust external* ***support system****, proactively protecting your* ***mental sanctuary****, and facing down internal roadblocks like* ***imposter syndrome*** *and perfectionism. Your well-being is the engine of your research.*

10

The supervisor partnership

In **Part I** of *The PhD Scholar's Compass,* we focused on the internal work: grounding your purpose, battling burnout, and decoding the often-brutal unwritten rules of academic culture. You learned that managing your emotional response and understanding the terrain are crucial for survival.

Now, as we transition into **Part II: The resilience core-partnership and well-being**, we must confront the central relationship that dictates your journey: **The supervisor partnership**.

Your supervisor is more than just a mentor; they are a **gatekeeper, a professional sponsor, and, eventually, a lifelong colleague.** This singular relationship holds the most influence over your stress levels, productivity, funding, and career trajectory. The goal of this chapter is to give you the strategic tools to transition this hierarchical relationship from one of dependence to one of long-term, symbiotic alliance.

The symbiotic ideal: Green flags in the partnership

The healthiest supervisor relationship is a working partnership built on mutual respect and shared, clearly defined goals. It is an alliance where both parties contribute expertise. These **Green flags** signal that your relationship is thriving and sustainable:

- **Clear expectations:** A good relationship operates with consistency. Your supervisor has a documented, preferred method for communication (e.g., "Email is fine, but I only check it fully on Tuesday and Thursday mornings") and a standard for drafts (e.g., "Send a max of 5,000 words, formatted using LaTex/MS Word"). This clarity drastically reduces your anxiety about *how* to engage them, protecting your focus time.

- **Psychological safety:** You can be intellectually honest with them. This means you can admit, "I don't understand this methodology," or "I failed the experiment three times," without fear of emotional reprisal or feeling judged. This safety allows you to course-correct quickly, preventing major delays and fostering intellectual honesty.

- **Active advocacy:** Your supervisor uses their established professional capital to advance your career. They introduce you to senior scholars at conferences, proactively forward funding or grant opportunities, and nominate you for internal awards. They are investing their *social sponsorship* in you, signaling deep belief in your potential.

- **Respect for boundaries:** They recognize you are a person, not just a research arm. They respect designated non-working hours and avoid sending non-urgent emails late at night. This practice protects your recovery time and mitigates the destructive 24/7 expectation trap.

Sources of strain: Red flags that degrade the relationship

Relationships aren't always a smooth sail and often break down due to inconsistency, a lack of advocacy, or a misuse of the power dynamic. Recognizing these **Red flags** early is crucial for self-preservation and for initiating necessary course correction.

- **The Ghost:** This occurs when your supervisor is consistently unresponsive to time-sensitive emails (e.g., grant submissions, conference deadlines), sometimes for weeks at end. The hidden cost is immense anxiety and missed opportunities.

  Proactive Response: *After a week, send a brief, non-accusatory follow-up:*

  "Re-sending this for visibility as the deadline for [Conference Name] is approaching on [Date]. If you can't review the full draft manuscript, please let me know which 5 pages I should prioritize for urgent feedback."

- **The Micromanager:** They over-edit simple emails, demand constant, trivial updates, or insist on methodology changes without offering a clear, data-driven rationale. This stifles your growth into an independent scholar.

  Proactive Response: *In your next meeting, state your need for independence:*

  "I need to focus on developing more independent writing and project management skills. Could we agree that for the next draft, I will send you only the argument and results sections for high-level feedback, and I'll manage the details of the literature review myself?"

- **The Absentee:** They consistently miss or cancel your scheduled check-ins, delegate your core mentorship entirely to a post-doc or junior colleague, and never seem to read your work carefully.

  Proactive Response: *Ask for a dedicated strategy meeting:*

  "I need to ensure my trajectory is solid for my Confirmation of Candidature. Can we schedule 90 minutes next month to map out my milestones for the next XX months and define a clear check-in cadence based on those goals?"

- **The Credit harvester:** They expect co-authorship (or, invite arbitrary collaborators to be listed as co-authors) on projects where their contribution does not meet the established academic criteria or push you to abandon your dissertation work for their irrelevant, large grant projects.

> Proactive Response: *Use a polite yet affirmative response, anchoring your time to your dissertation:*
> *"Thank you for the opportunity, but given the critical timeline for my core dissertation data collection this quarter, I need to focus exclusively on that project."*

Managing the partnership across the PhD lifecycle

A long-lasting, symbiotic relationship is actively managed across three distinct phases of your career.

Phase 1: Before the PhD – The partnership contract

Choosing a supervisor should be treated like entering a professional contract. The **fit of management style** is often more important for your mental health than the exact alignment of research topics.

Action Point: The operational interview

Before accepting a position, ask these operational questions to clearly define the working rules:

- **Communication style:** "What is your preferred channel for quick questions (email, chat, office drop-in)?" and, critically, **"What is your expected turnaround time for reviewing a standard chapter draft?"**

- **Boundaries & urgency:** "Do you prefer scheduled check-ins, or are they ad-hoc?" and "What is the best way to contact you for a **true emergency** on a weekend or holiday?" (This subtly establishes that weekend contact is strictly for emergencies.)
- **Autonomy:** "How do you balance guiding the project's scope versus allowing the student intellectual freedom to innovate or pivot?"

We have already looked into this in a lot more detail in **Chapter 4- Vetting your future supervisor** in Part-I of this book.

Phase 2: During the PhD – The periodic review

During the core years of the PhD, the relationship must be reviewed and tuned regularly. Your role shifts, and the project scope changes.

Action Point: The quarterly alignment document

Twice a semester (or, a similar sustainable frequency), prepare a simple, shared document for your meeting. This transforms your check-ins from reactive problem-solving sessions to focused, strategic planning:

- **Last quarter's achievement:** *List 3-5 concrete outputs (e.g., Draft of Chapter 2 submitted; IRB/Ethics approved, XX manuscripts under review/published).*
- **Next quarter's focus:** *List 3-5 concrete milestones (e.g., Draft 75% of Chapter 3; Submit abstract to Major Conference).*

- **Potential roadblocks & support needs:** *Identify specific areas where you need their help (e.g., I need a letter of support for a grant; I require feedback on my statistical analysis plan by [Date]).*

This practice helps the supervisor to address timelines aligned with your goals and their workload, removes ambiguity, and proves you are managing the project like a professional while respecting the commitments of both parties.

Phase 3: After the PhD – The colleague transition

The ultimate goal is to transition the supervisor from *boss* to *colleague* for life. This process begins the moment you defend and step into your professional role.

Action Point: The professional pivot

Once you have your doctorate in hand, consciously shift the dynamic by initiating mutually beneficial professional actions, rather than only asking for favors or letters of recommendation:

1. **Offer expertise first:** Instead of asking, "Do you have any jobs for me?" try, "I saw that new paper by Scholar X. If you or your new students are interested in replicating that analysis, I'd be happy to share my code and methods with you."
2. **Provide resources:** Introduce your supervisor to a relevant junior scholar or colleague you met at a new institution, framing it as a professional connection for

them.

3. **Share success:** Keep them casually updated on your career wins (job offers, major grants, book contracts) without excessive detail. This reinforces their identity as your sponsor and maintains the professional bond.

Contingency planning: Handling conflict and escalation

Conflict(s) will arise, often from intellectual misalignment—disagreements over project scope, methodology, or interpretation and at times may not be easily resolvable. Yet, handling these effectively builds respect, proving you are ready for independent scholarship.

The art of intellectual disagreement

When a supervisor proposes an idea you believe will derail your project, do not respond with anxiety or personal preference. Respond with **evidence**. Your job is to present a strong, evidenced case for your choice, turning a potential conflict into a productive scholarly discussion.

Strategy: The evidence-backed counter-proposal

1. **Acknowledge and validate (The 'Yes'):** Start by validating their underlying point. *"I see your concern about the current sample size, and I agree we need to strengthen the power of the analysis."*

2. **Present the problem (The 'But'):** Introduce the practical constraint using data or time. *"But collecting the additional 50 participants would delay my submission by six months, forcing me to miss the critical hiring cycle."*

3. **Propose the data-backed solution (The 'Therefore'):** Offer your alternative solution, backed by external academic literature. *"Therefore, based on the simulation study by Dr. [Scholar Name] in 20XX, I propose we use a Bayesian approach instead of a Frequentist one, which offers sufficient power with the current N, keeping us on track for a timely defense."*

Though, this can be easier said than done. There may be times where you and your advisor may not come to a consensus. Then what? Can you bypass your supervisor? Yes, but there are risks as we discussed in **Chapter 8- Decoding the unwritten rules of academic culture.**

Beyond the primary partnership: Cultivating your network

While the supervisor is the anchor of your professional life, they cannot—and should not—be your only source of support. Relying solely on one mentor creates a single point of failure and often places an unfair emotional burden on your supervisor. Your goal is to build a mentorship network that functions like a personal board of directors.

The proactive management strategies in this chapter were designed to build a robust partnership with your anchor mentor. With your central professional relationship managed, it's time to expand your defenses. In the next chapter, we look at the full architecture of your well-being, from peer groups to family communication, and map out the necessary steps for **building a robust support system**.

11

Building a robust support system

Chapter 10 focused on actively managing your singular, most critical academic relationship—the one with your supervisor- the anchor mentor. You learned how to spot green and red flags, professionalize that partnership and why it's essential to cultivate additional voices in your life, recognizing that no single person can meet all your needs.

This chapter shifts from managing a relationship to **building an architecture of support**—a resilient system designed to catch you when the inevitable academic or personal setbacks occur. A robust support system is your greatest defense against burnout and isolation; it's the difference between powering through a difficult quarter and completely stalling out.

The power of peers: Mutual accountability and shared struggle

Your peers are your greatest and most immediate allies. No one understands the unique, sometimes absurd, struggles of a PhD quite like another PhD scholar, especially those facing the same departmental pressures or methodologies. The moments of shared struggle are the foundation for a professional, durable peer network. So, does that mean that you should connect with peers only within your Department and domain? Not quite...

Why network beyond your lab?

While your immediate lab mates or cohort are valuable, your external peers—scholars in different departments, programs, or even universities—offer a unique advantage: **unbiased psychological safety.** They can offer emotional support and career advice without the complicating factor of departmental hierarchy or competition for the same resources. Expanding your circle breaks the "golden handcuffs" of your lab and gives you a broader perspective on the academic job market. So, what should you look for when building such a peer network?

Building peer networks for growth

Building this peer network should focus on both emotional support and tangible professional progress:

- ***Shared accountability***: Find one or two trusted peers to establish a "weekly check-in" cadence. This involves briefly sharing three things: Progress Made (last week's wins), Goal Set (this week's target), and Roadblock (a specific challenge to overcome). This simple routine breaks down inertia and forces you to articulate your progress.

- ***Writing groups (Non-critical)***: These are not critique sessions. A writing group provides a shared, quiet block of time where you and your peers commit to working on individual tasks (data analysis, reading, writing). The collective commitment provides powerful motivation. Over the decades of mentoring scholars around the globe, I've seen some mentees adopt this while others work better in their own time and space. Hence, this is non-critical but an option should you choose to adopt it.

- ***Honest feedback***: Peers are often better equipped than supervisors to provide candid, real-world feedback on presentation styles, conference talks, or practice job interviews, as they are closer to the stage you are currently navigating.

Now that you understand what are the key foundational pillars of a peer network, you must be wondering, so, who do I add to this network? In what follows, we categorize the types of peers and identify their key roles in your growth journey.

Mentors, sponsors, and allies: Expanding your circle of influence

Relying solely on your supervisor for all advice, advocacy, and encouragement is unrealistic and professionally limiting. It's vital to recognize and intentionally cultivate three distinct roles that together form your professional board of directors.

The three key peer roles:

- **The Mentor: (Gives advice)** This person is typically more experienced and offers wisdom, perspective, and general guidance on career paths and skills development. They answer the question: "How should I approach this problem?"

Example: A senior faculty member who advises you on which journals to target or how to balance teaching with research.

- **The Sponsor: (Gives access)** This person is actively advocating for you, often behind closed doors, spending their professional capital to advance your career. They answer the question: "Who should I be talking to?"

Example: A senior industry researcher who recommends you for a specific grant or a conference organizer who pushes for you to get a coveted speaking slot.

- **The Ally: (Gives support)** This person supports you personally and emotionally. They may or may not be in academia, but they provide a safe space and unconditional encouragement. They answer the question: "Are you doing okay?"

Example: A colleague who gives you a pep talk after a rejection or a friend who brings you coffee before a big defense.

There may be a chance that you may find a supervisor or a peer fitting more than one of these roles but either way, your peer network (imagine them as your Board of Directors directing your PhD journey) should have these pillar roles fulfilled for your growth. But, assembling a peer crew is one thing, how do keep them engaged in your journey from Day 0 to PhD defense day?

Strategic cultivation: Practical do's and don'ts

To effectively engage your support network, you must be proactive and professional in your approach.

Intentional networking (The Do's)

- Do **offer value** first. Share a relevant article, offer to help them organize a small event, or ask an informed question about their work. Relationships are reciprocal.
- Do make your **asks specific**. Instead of "Can we chat about my career?" ask, "I'm applying for the [Specific Post-Doc], could you review my statement of purpose?"
- Do **express gratitude** and close the loop. Send a brief

email thanking them for their time and letting them know the positive outcome of their advice.

Common pitfalls to avoid (The Don'ts)

- Don't assume a **mentor will do your work for you**. Always come with a specific, articulated problem and 2-3 potential solutions for them to weigh in on.
- Don't **expect them to read 50+ pages** of work. Reserve large draft reading for your supervisor or committee. Keep requests to external mentors focused and bite-sized.
- Don't **neglect to communicate**. If you take their advice, tell them it worked. If you chose a different path, let them know why—this shows respect for their time.

If you assemble your dream team- the Board, it is up to you to keep them engaged throughout and make them feel valued. Both you and your Board must have skin in the game- to help you get to the finish line and see you win. Otherwise, you just assembled cheerleaders with no stakes in your growth.

The home front: Communicating your needs to friends and family

Managing a professional peer network is one thing but there are also critical relationships that one needs to manage beyond academia- the friends and family. This is especially important if you are pursuing a PhD abroad, thousands of miles away from home.

For friends and family outside of academia, the PhD is often a mystery. They might not understand why you can't just "take a day off," why your schedule is irregular, or why you're so exhausted even after working from home. This lack of understanding can turn otherwise supportive relationships into a source of stress.

The key to preserving these vital relationships is **proactive communication and setting realistic expectations.**

- Translate your work: Avoid academic jargon. Instead of saying, "I'm finalizing the methodology section for the structural equation model," say, "I have a tight deadline this week to write the instructions for the final set of experiments."

- Define your time: Establish and communicate "protected work blocks" and "protected rest blocks." Say, "I'm completely unavailable from 9 AM to 5 PM, but I'm yours from 5 PM until bedtime." This clear boundary prevents the passive-aggressive expectation that because you're home, you're available.

- Manage emotional spillage: Share your wins and progress, not just your crises. If you only talk about the problems, your family will assume the PhD is a purely negative experience. Share the excitement of a new finding or a successfully defended proposal.

Tool: The "Communicating your needs" framework

When you feel stressed or misunderstood, it's easy to slip into accusatory language, which triggers defensiveness and shuts down the support channel. As a PhD scholar, you have very limited support channel so you should treat your true friends and family as critical currency that should be respected and rationed and not forgotten.

The simplest and most powerful framework for communicating your needs without causing conflict is the **"I" Statement.**

This framework uses a simple structure: "I feel X when Y because Z, and I need A." Instead of accusatory language (Blaming the other person) like:

"You don't understand how busy I am, why are you calling right now?"

"You never ask about my research, you clearly don't care."

"Why can't you ever take the kids for the whole day?"

Try This (The I-statement approach):

Example 1: Setting work boundaries

"I feel overwhelmed when my workday is interrupted because I lose my focus and momentum. I need a boundary where we only talk after 7 PM tonight."

Example 2: Seeking emotional support

"I feel isolated when I don't share my work, and I need you to let me talk for five minutes about my latest chapter tonight so I can feel supported."

Example 3: Asking for help/time

"I am feeling depleted from working on this grant all week. I need you to take the kids this Saturday morning so I can recharge and be a better partner/parent later."

This tool reframes the conversation around your internal state and needs, ensuring your personal relationships remain a source of strength, not stress.

By expanding your network with peers for accountability, cultivating strategic sponsors for advocacy, and communicating effectively on the home front using the **"I" Statement** framework, you have successfully built a robust external fortress. This system is your first and strongest line of defense, ensuring that you have multiple sources of professional advice and personal support to endure the PhD journey. You are no longer reliant on a single relationship; your resilience is now distributed across a strong, professional network.

However, even the most formidable external armor cannot fully protect you from the internal psychological toll of the PhD. The pressure to produce results, the inevitable rejections, and the pervasive culture of overwork can silently erode your motivation and sense of self-worth.

The next critical step is to turn inward. In **Chapter 12: Your mind, your sanctuary**, we will focus on internal defenses, addressing the pervasive **guilt** that accompanies taking a break, the urgent need to decouple your personal identity from your research outcomes, and why treating mental rest as a mandatory professional task is essential for long-term survival.

12

Your mind, your sanctuary

You've built your external fortress in Chapter 11—a network of peers and sponsors designed to guide and support your professional journey. But now, it's time to confront the greatest threat to your PhD: **internal collapse.**

The academic environment is uniquely toxic to mental well-being, often due to unspoken pressures that few outside the ivory tower fully appreciate. The **explicit sources** of stress—*harsh feedback, failed experiments, brutal rejection cycles,* and an often-*ambiguous finish line*—are continually compounded by **implicit sources** like *chronic professional isolation,* the *unhealthy fusion of self-worth with project success,* and the ever-present, silent killer of **impostor syndrome**. This convergence leads to one of academia's highest attrition factors: deep, chronic burnout. Neglecting your mental health is not a minor inconvenience; it **guarantees derailment**, jeopardizing years of work and causing long-term emotional and professional harm. Therefore, the care of your mind is not a soft skill or a reward you earn after finishing your work, but the most fundamental form of professional resilience you possess—it is mandatory.

This chapter is dedicated to building your internal sanctuary, equipping you with the tools to manage the daily psychological load. We will begin by addressing the deep-seated **guilt** that accompanies taking a break and establishing a framework for mandatory rest.

The guilt trap: Reclassifying rest as resilience not failure

One of the greatest psychological challenges of the PhD is the feeling that if you're not actively working, you're failing or, falling behind. This pervasive sense of guilt turns necessary rest into a stressor, leading to incomplete recovery, reduced productivity and eventually, burnout.

The myth of constant productivity

You are a human being, not a machine. Your brain requires downtime to consolidate memories, process complex information, and generate new ideas (a process known as the **Default Mode Network**). Thinking of rest as a luxury or a reward is fundamentally incorrect; it is a **mandatory input** for high-quality, sustainable work.

Taking guilt-free breaks

To overcome the guilt, you must actively reframe your definition of a break:

- **Active rest (The recharge):** These are activities that engage a different part of your brain or body, generating energy rather than consuming it. Examples include exercise, cooking, socializing, or learning a new, unrelated hobby.
- **Passive rest (The reset):** True downtime with minimal sensory input. This includes napping, gentle meditation, or simply staring out the window. This is critical for recovering from deep cognitive labor.

A well-scheduled break is a **productive decision**, not a moment of weakness. It prevents errors, refreshes perspective, and ensures the hours you *do* spend working are maximally effective.

Identity, worth, and the stigma of failure

What people rarely talk about is how the PhD demands that you fuse your personal identity with your professional output. When your experiment fails or your paper is rejected, it doesn't just feel like professional criticism—it feels like a rejection of *You*.

Decoupling self-worth from research outcomes:

1. **Acknowledge the process:** Remind yourself that re-

jection is endemic to the system, not a measure of your worth. A failed experiment is data; a rejected paper is an opportunity for revision. **Your value as a human is separate from your citation count.**

2. **Use external anchors:** Maintain hobbies, friendships, or volunteer work outside of academia. These external anchors prove that your identity is multi-faceted and prevents the PhD from becoming the single, fragile column supporting your sense of self.
3. **The two identities:** Learn to differentiate between the **scholar identity** (which is learning, failing, and dependent on supervisors) and the **professional identity** (the subject matter expert who owns their work). This separation allows you to critique your *work* without attacking your *self*.

Recognizing the warning signs

It's crucial to distinguish between normal academic stress and genuine burnout or mental health crisis. Burnout is a specific syndrome characterized by three dimensions: **Exhaustion, Cynicism, and Reduced efficacy.**

If you notice these shifts lasting for more than a few weeks, it's time to take serious action:

- **Exhaustion:** Feeling constantly drained, physically or mentally, even after sleeping.
- **Cynicism (or Depersonalization):** An increased sense

of detachment from your job, your colleagues, and the value of your research. You may feel overwhelmingly negative about your field.

- **Reduced efficacy:** A decline in your confidence and a sense of professional accomplishment. Tasks that were once easy now seem impossible.

Normalizing professional help

Despite the high rates of anxiety, depression, and burnout among PhD students, seeking help still carries a stigma. Treat your mental health with the same seriousness you treat a physical ailment. Utilizing campus counseling services, finding a therapist, or speaking with a doctor about chronic stress are acts of strength and self-preservation, not failure. They are essential tools for professional sustainability as a walk in woods or trek to the mountains may not always suffice.

Protecting your inner sanctuary is the most advanced form of productivity. However, there is one last internal battle to win before you can fully apply structure to your work: the fight against self-doubt. The highest-performing scholars often face the most persistent emotional blockades. We turn now to **Chapter 13: Imposter syndrome and perfectionism**, to dismantle the mental habits that can still paralyze a scholar, even one who has built a strong support core.

13

Imposter syndrome and perfectionism

You have thus far learned how to manage the working relationship with your supervisor (Chapter 10), built a robust support system (Chapter 11) and established your mental boundaries (Chapter 12). Your inner sanctuary is now protected.

Yet, even the most prepared scholar can be paralyzed by self-doubt, leading to procrastination and non-submission. This is the last internal battle of the PhD journey: the fight against **imposter syndrome** and its co-conspirator, **perfectionism**. These two emotional forces are not signs of weakness; they are the occupational hazards of high intelligence and high expectations. They must be managed as strategically as any data set.

The imposter syndrome epidemic

Imposter syndrome is the feeling that *you are a fraud who has fooled everyone* into believing you are competent, and that any moment, you will be "*found out.*" In the PhD environment, this feeling is epidemic because the system is designed to constantly expose the limits of your knowledge.

The more you learn, the more you realize the vastness of what you do not know. This is the **PhD paradox**. You are surrounded by world experts, and your job is to critique and advance their work, which only amplifies the feeling of inadequacy.

Tool: The success journal

To fight a feeling, you need facts. The success journal tool (previously discussed in **Chapter 8- Decoding the unwritten rules of academic culture**) is a simple, non-negotiable tool for logging factual evidence of your competence and fighting imposter syndrome effectively.

Perfectionism: The trap of non-submission

> *I will submit the manuscript when it is perfect.*

Does this claim sound familiar? I bet you have a manuscript sitting in your drafts waiting to reach "perfection" before you hit submit.

Perfectionism is often misunderstood as having high standards. In the context of a PhD, true perfectionism is the paralyzing fear that your work is not ready, leading to **non-submission**. You refine the introduction for the tenth time while the conclusion remains unwritten. Perfectionism is the biggest cause of project delay because the work is never "good enough" to leave your computer.

This paralyzing fear also manifests as "**productive procrastination.**" A classic, self-soothing habit for the stressed scholar is the urge to **re-arrange or clean the desk**. This activity *feels* productive—it involves physical motion, organization, and results in a visible output (a clean desk)—but it is a low-value task that simply **avoids** the high-anxiety task of writing or complex analysis. Recognize this habit for what it is: an avoidance mechanism, not actual productivity.

Tool: The 80% rule of submission

The academic world, particularly your supervisor, requires a draft to give you feedback. They cannot give feedback on work that only exists in your head. Adopt the **80% Rule**:

- The goal is to produce a well-structured, coherent draft that is **80% complete and accurate**. The remaining 20%—the polishing, the nuance, the flawless formatting—will be achieved *through* the feedback process, not before it.
- A draft that is 80% complete and submitted is 100% more useful than a draft that is 99% complete but never seen.

- Recognize that your supervisor's job is to critique. If they find no flaws, you didn't give them enough to work with. Treat the red pen as a helpful dialogue, not an indictment of your intelligence.

Remember a manuscript on your desk is of no use to anyone and is going to collect dust. So, how do you prevent that from happening?

The minimum viable chapter (MVC)

Break the chapter into the smallest possible unit you can realistically submit. This strategy is borrowed from software development, prioritizing iteration over pre-perfection.

- Define your MVC as a section, a figure, or a two-page literature review summary.
- The goal is to produce a low-stakes, *submit-able* item that requires less than 4 hours of focused work.
- Submit the MVC, ask for specific feedback on it, and immediately move to the next MVC. This constant, low-stakes submission trains your mind to move past the paralysis of a single, daunting "perfect chapter."

You have now completed **Part II: The resilience core—Partnership and well-being**. You moved from managing the critical supervisor relationship and building a robust external support system to fortifying your internal world against burnout, imposter syndrome, and paralysis.

You have oriented your compass (Part I) and built your psychological and relational armor (Part II). You now possess the necessary intellectual awareness, stamina, and support structure to survive the marathon. The final stage is execution. In **Part III: Setting up your bearings**, we move from psychological preparation to the tactical tools you need to manage your time, plan your research, and execute your Masterful Research Question, shifting your identity from a diligent student to a prolific, published scholar with a bold vision.

III

Setting your bearings – Strategic navigation in academia

Having anchored your purpose and built your resilience, Part III is about pure execution. This section provides the tactical blueprint for navigating the academic life. We cover strategic time management, efficient literature review, research design (Masterful Research Question, methodology, financial planning), navigating the proposal defense, and the entire process of data management, analysis, and writing your core dissertation chapters. Set your bearings for efficient completion.

14

Strategic time and energy management

The difference between a stressed scholar and a productive, sustainable scholar isn't about working longer; it's about working smarter by managing **energy**, not just time. Time is finite, but your energy fluctuates. This chapter gives you the tools to align your most demanding tasks with your peak energy states, moving beyond simple scheduling to true strategic deployment of your cognitive resources.

Mastering your ultradian rhythm: The 90-minute focus cycle

The pomodoro technique (25 minutes on, 5 minutes off) is a good starting point, but it ignores a fundamental biological fact: your brain operates on an **ultradian rhythm**. This is a 90 to 120-minute cycle of peak concentration followed by a natural dip, a pattern that repeats throughout the day. True focus lasts about 90 minutes. Trying to push past that natural break is where diminishing returns and mental fatigue set in.

Instead of rigidly adhering to 25 minutes, use this natural cycle to structure your deep work sessions. Commit to 90 minutes of **deep work** (writing, data analysis, complex reading) followed by a mandatory 20-30 minute break that involves **physical movement** (walking, stretching) to reset the cognitive slate.

Tool: The personal energy inventory

To master this rhythm, you first need to understand your unique energy profile. This tool is not a schedule, but a journal you keep for one week to track your flow. For every major activity, log the following three factors:

- **Time and chronotype:** The exact time of day you performed the task (e.g., 9:00 am - 10:30 am).
- **Cognitive load:** Was the task high-stakes (creative, analytical) or low-stakes (administrative, repetitive)?
- **Energy post-activity:** On a scale of 1 to 5, how energized or drained did you feel immediately after the task?

Actionable insight: This inventory will reveal your **chronotype** (are you a morning lark or a night owl?) and your most effective **deep work windows**. Schedule high-cognitive tasks (analysis, writing) exclusively in these windows. Reserve low-cognitive tasks (emails, meeting prep, formatting) for your lower-energy periods.

And, don't listen to advice like "You should come to lab and work from 5:00AM) or similar. You should work aligned with your most productive slots as everyone has their own personal energy inventory.

But, now that you know your energy inventory, how do you ration it out to make the most of it? The answer- cognitive batching.

The art of cognitive batching: Eliminating switch cost

Firstly, let's demystify **multi-tasking**. Every time we've asked a mentee to define it, they inevitably say something along the lines of "doing multiple tasks simultaneously". This is ridiculous and fundamentally flawed- multi-tasking isn't meant to be taken in literal sense. You have one brain, you are a human and not an Octopus. This is absolutely not how multi-tasking works and knowing how it does is crucial for **cognitive batching**.

So, multi-tasking basically means making staggered progress across multiple tasks. Meaning, this is a round robin approach- you allocate time to a task to make some progress and when that window is up, you switch to another task. Like this, you diversify your chances of success by staggering your progress across multiple tasks, all contributing to your overall PhD progress. But, there is a caveat. How do you pick up the next task? Is there no effect on your productivity if you pick the next task at random?

The task switching caveat with multi-tasking

Every time you switch from one type of task (e.g., writing a literature review) to a fundamentally different one (e.g., coding data analysis), your brain pays a **switching cost**. This mental friction wastes time and drains energy. The secret to efficiency is **cognitive batching**: grouping tasks that require the same mental state.

The trap of pseudo-activity syndrome

Before you implement task batching, you must address the deeper issue of **pseudo-activity syndrome**. This is the habit of confusing low-value busyness with meaningful progress. As discussed in the previous chapter, perfectionism often leads to procrastinating on high-stakes tasks (like drafting a tough section) by substituting a comfortable, low-stakes task (like rearranging your desk, formatting references, or reading emails). **Pseudo-activity syndrome** means doing *just about anything* is confused with doing *something meaningful* for your core research progress.

The cognitive and emotional satisfaction of checking off a simple, administrative task is addictive, but it's not helpful. The purpose of cognitive batching is not just to reduce the switching cost between tasks, but to ensure that your **Creation Block**—your high-value time—is completely free from the lure of pseudo-activity.

Strategy: Task grouping by cognitive load

Create four distinct blocks (add more only if you can manage the increased cognitive load!!) in your week and only perform the designated task type during that scheduled time. These blocks separate the mental muscles required for different types of work.

1. **Creation block (High cognitive load):** Exclusively for generating new content. This means drafting chapters, running complex simulations, or developing new theoretical models.
   Motto: generate.

2. **Consumption block (Medium cognitive load):** Exclusively for intake and synthesis. This includes deep, focused reading of journal articles, annotating sources, and reviewing feedback from your supervisor.
   Motto: absorb.

3. **Administration block (Low cognitive load):** Exclusively for necessary but non-core tasks. This covers email, scheduling, preparing slide decks, formatting references, and paying bills. Batch these to one or two slots per day.
   Motto: tidy.

4. **Data block (Variable load):** Dedicated time for organizing, cleaning, and analyzing your specific data. If the analysis is complex, treat this as a high-cognitive load creation block. If it's routine cleaning, treat it as low.

Motto: process.

The rule: Never allow a task from one block to bleed into another's scheduled time. If a writing session runs into your administration block, you stop writing and start the admin task. This trains your focus and reduces decision fatigue and follow a strategic to-do list.

The only challenge is that to-do list is a passive tool and you need something more proactive to keep you focused and motivated throughout your journey, cue- The Done List.

The Done list add-on for success journal: Motivation multiplier

The PhD is an infinite project; you are never truly "done" until you pass the defense. This psychological reality can crush motivation. The **Done list** is your daily and weekly counter-narrative.

- **What it is:** a running record of every small success, written down immediately after completion. This includes non-obvious wins like "successfully debugged the code," "sent one email i was dreading," or "read and annotated one difficult chapter."

- **Why it works:** the done list is concrete proof of cumulative progress. When **imposter syndrome** or **burnout** strikes, you can look back and see the sheer volume of work you have accomplished, restoring your sense of capability and fighting the feeling that you are spinning your wheels. It shifts your focus from the massive work ahead to the undeniable victories behind you.

The **Done list** and the **Success journal** (previously introduced in Chapters 8,13) essentially operate as a unified system to combat self-doubt and build resilience. The **Done list** is your daily, **tactical ledger** for tracking **output**—every task completed, meeting attended, or page written is objective proof that you were productive. The **Success journal** is the weekly, **psychological record** used to validate your **competence** as a scholar. The essential step is taking the factual accomplishments from your daily Done List (e.g., "Finished data cleaning") and consciously logging them in the Journal as evidence of your rigor and value, thus translating immediate effort into sustained self-worth to resist imposter syndrome and stay motivated.

So, you now know your energy inventory, you understand how to multi-task and how to batch tasks with similar cognitive load while documenting a done list to maximize productivity. But, how do you enforce this system and prevent external elements from derailing you?

The physics of boundaries: Preventing time leakage

Building on the internal commitment to rest as discussed in Chapter 7, this is about the external, practical enforcement of those commitments. **Time leakage** occurs when vague boundaries allow low-priority work to siphon time from high-priority rest or deep work.

Here are three external enforcement strategies:

- **The shutdown ritual:** schedule the final 15 minutes of your workday for a **shutdown ritual**. This is where you clean your desk, organize your files, and write the three most important tasks for the *next* day. When the ritual is complete, you are officially done. This prevents residual thinking about work.

- **Mute by intention:** move all messaging apps (slack, whatsapp, etc.) to a second home screen or folder on your phone. **Mute all non-essential channels** and only check them during your scheduled administration block. If it's not a true emergency (which is rare), it can wait.

- **Physical boundary cues:** use a clear **"deep work in progress" sign** on your office door or desk (even at home). This external cue signals to partners, colleagues, and family that your 90-minute block is non-negotiable, turning an internal intention into an external expectation.

By viewing your energy as a limited resource and deploying it strategically, you convert the chaotic, draining PhD process into a structured, sustainable career path. You are now equipped with the tools to protect your most valuable cognitive assets and maintain consistent motivation. However, all the time management in the world is useless if you are spending those protected hours doing inefficient work. Like what you ask?

The biggest time sink for almost every scholar is the initial phase of research and writing: the dreaded never ending literature review. Knowing how to protect the time is only half the battle; the other half is knowing how to make the work count. Next chapter dives into the specific, advanced techniques needed to streamline your intake of academic sources, ensuring every hour spent reading is a productive one.

15

The art of efficient literature review

In Chapter 14, we established the fundamental building blocks of a sustainable PhD: protecting your **deep work windows**, managing your energy (not just time), and celebrating progress with a **done list**. You now know how to create non-negotiable hours for your research.

But protecting the time is only half the battle. If you fill those hard-won, distraction-free hours with an inefficient process, you still lose. The most significant efficiency risk for any early-stage scholar lies in the **literature review**. This phase is where dedicated hours can vanish into an **infinite loop** of reading that yields little tangible progress. The stack of unread or half-read papers on your desk doesn't count as much as you'd like. This chapter provides the strategic framework to convert that chaos into clarity, ensuring your protected deep work time is used for **synthesis and contribution**, not passive consumption.

The problem: Confronting the infinite reading cycle

For the early-stage scholar, the literature review phase—the first major intellectual hurdle—is often the most dreaded. The problem isn't the reading itself, but the lack of an endpoint. Unlike an experimental phase with a set protocol, the literature review feels like an **infinite loop**. There is a sea of research material out there already with more getting pumped on a daily if not hourly basis.

You are constantly haunted by the question: **Have I read enough? When does this end?** This feeling of being perpetually behind is what makes the phase so draining. Without a structured system, the goal shifts from *framing your research* to simply *acquiring more articles*, a habit that maximizes anxiety and minimizes actual dissertation progress. You must replace the goal of **comprehension** with the goal of **contribution**.

The solution: The dynamic digital literature review database

You cannot manage an infinite process with passive tools like folders of PDFs or static bibliographies or worse, scribbled notes over print outs. To transition out of the reading loop, you need a single, centralized database that forces you to **process, synthesize, and immediately extract the gap** from every paper you read.

This database, which you should maintain in a tool like

Notion, Airtable, or even an advanced spreadsheet, is not just a reference manager; it is your **dissertation blueprint**.

Key components of the dynamic database

This is a living (digital) document that is **dynamically updated** as you read. The structure shifts your focus from the paper's *content* to the paper's *utility* for your project.

- **Citation & link:** Standard bibliographic information and a direct link to the article.

- **Core contribution:** What is the single, most important finding of this paper? (1-2 sentences only).

- **Methodology & data:** What specific method or data did they use? (e.g., used LSTM on stock market data from 2008-2018).

- **Limitations & gaps:** Where did the authors admit they fell short? What did they say they *couldn't* do? (Crucial for gap spotting).

- **Project's connection:** How will I cite or use this paper? (e.g., provides baseline model, justifies data selection, or serves as a direct critique).

- **Thematic keywords:** 3-5 keywords for finding themes (e.g., 'causality', 'temporal shift', 'lstm').

While categorizing the knowledge using the key components

listed above helps keep your database manageable and for you to know what you are reading and the why behind it, not every published work is to be treated with equal rigor. Let's look into how one makes the literature review an iterative process.

The AI shortcut: A word of caution

In your quest for efficiency, you will undoubtedly be tempted by the explosion of AI-enabled literature review tools. These platforms promise to summarize thousands of papers, find gaps automatically, and even "chat" with your PDFs to extract data. While these tools can be powerful assistants for discovery, they present a significant risk to the burgeoning scholar: ***the temptation to cut intellectual corners.***

The danger of outsourced thinking

A PhD is not just a test of your ability to aggregate information; it is a test of your **critical synthesis**. When you rely solely on an AI to summarize a paper or identify a gap, you are outsourcing the very "mental muscle" you are supposed to be building.

- **Hallucinations and nuance:** AI summaries often miss the subtle "intellectual tension" mentioned earlier. They can misinterpret a limitation or, worse, fabricate a finding (hallucinate) that sounds plausible but doesn't exist in the data.

- **The loss of serendipity:** Part of the literature review strategy is the ability to spot a peripheral connection that an AI, programmed for direct relevance, might ignore.

- **Superficial mastery:** If you haven't struggled with the text yourself, you will be unable to defend your "gap" during your candidacy or final defense. A reviewer will quickly spot if your understanding is based on a 200-word AI summary rather than a rigorous engagement with the methodology.

The golden rule for ethically adopting AI in research

Use AI for **discovery**, never for **validation**. Use it to find potentially relevant papers you might have missed, but do not allow an AI to fill your *dynamic literature review database* for you. The entries in your database—especially the "Project's connection" column—must be the result of your own cognitive processing.

True efficiency is not about reading less; it is about ensuring that what you do read is processed with a level of critical depth that no algorithm can yet replicate.

Now, let's look into a strategy for optimizing the literature review process with iterative passes.

The wide vs. deep strategy: Optimizing your reading passes

Remember how we talked about strategic time and energy management previously. Those principles apply to sifting through literature as well.

An early-stage scholar is often tempted to read every published work line-by-line, wasting precious time and energy. The key to efficiency is realizing that **90% of papers only deserve a 10% reading effort.** You need a strategy to decide when to go **Wide** (many papers, little detail) versus **Deep** (few papers, high rigor).

Pass 1: Going wide (The 5-minute scan)

The goal of the first pass is to rapidly determine if the paper is a **core competitor** or just **contextual noise**. You are not seeking deep comprehension; you are hunting for keywords and database entries to only include relevant works and here is how you do this.

- **Title and keywords**: Does it match your research domain? If not, discard.

- **Abstract**: Get the core contribution, problem, and solution. If the problem/solution is irrelevant, discard.

- **Conclusion & future work**: This is the most valuable section. The conclusion shows what the authors did, and the Future Work section explicitly lists their Limitations & Gaps. This immediately fills your most critical database column.

- **Skim methods & experimental conditions**: Quickly identify the specific model, data set, or study population used. You need just enough detail to enter into your Methodology & Data column.

Action: If the paper passes the initial scan, you stop reading and immediately use the extracted information to fill the five key columns in your dynamic database. **Note:** How the sections are arranged for a quick grasp instead of following the chronology in which a published work is typically written. These jumps are necessary to quickly filter competitor from the noise.

Pass 2, 3, and beyond: Going deep (The rigorous review)

You only proceed to deep reading when a paper has been identified through Pass 1 as a **direct competitor** or a foundational work you plan to use as a **baseline model** or **direct critique**. This rigorous review is only for the select 5-10% of papers.

- Focus: Read the Methods section inside out for reproducibility, check statistical rigor, and scrutinize the experimental validation conditions.
- Goal: Read not for understanding, but for the ability to critique and replicate. This is where you test the paper's assumptions against your own evolving project goals.

Now that you know how to effectively read papers as you find them and when and how to screen them for addition to your literature review database, it's time to learn how make sense of the knowledge you just accumulated.

The shift from reading to synthesizing

By forcing yourself to complete the **limitations & gaps** and **my project's connection** fields for every paper, you achieve **two powerful things**:

1. **Active reading:** you are no longer passively absorbing text. You are actively hunting for weaknesses and opportunities, which is the definition of advanced scholarship.

2. **The exit condition:** you know you have read **enough** when your database is robust enough to fully support the argument in your *introduction chapter*. The decision to move to implementation is triggered not by the size of your pile of papers, but by the intellectual richness of your synthesis. When the limitations column starts repeating itself and you have clear evidence to support your proposed novelty, **you stop reading and start writing/implementing.**

But wait!! If you are pursuing a technical PhD such as in Robotics and Automation, I bet the moment I say "implement", you start imagining a code editor with lines of code ready to be messed with. But that's not it.

The implementation trap: Why coding must wait

There is a powerful, yet dangerous, temptation in computational and empirical disciplines: to immediately download the code, install the dependencies, and start running the models for every paper you read. **This is a horrible way to understand someone's work.**

The moment you start trying to reproduce results or adapt a paper's code, your cognitive focus irrevocably shifts:

1. **From contribution to bug fixing:** instead of spending your valuable research time contemplating the authors' intellectual contribution, limitations, and theoretical implications, you are now troubleshooting python version conflicts, dependency issues, and errors in someone else's codebase.

2. **Adds no novelty:** spending a week wrestling with a public repository to make it run adds zero novelty to your dissertation. You are simply debugging, a process that is time-consuming and often emotionally draining with little to no reward associated. Your PhD is not a master's course in software maintenance.

3. **Misdirected energy:** the precious mental energy you saved using the strategic time management techniques

from Chapter 14 is wasted on low-value, administrative coding tasks.

The rule: read, synthesize, and document the paper's contribution in your database **before** you touch any code. Implementation should only begin when you are ready to implement **your own novel addition**, not just the work of others and you have a shortlist of state of the art works you will be competing with.

So, you have now read and prepared your dynamic literature review database. You've iteratively added relevant works to it and it has grown sufficiently. The biggest question in your mind will be- How do you map all this information into the next action point? In other words, have you found your niche yet? Let's look into this right away.

The ultimate challenge: The art of gap spotting

The hardest task in the literature review is **gap spotting**. Your supervisor tells you to "find the gap" or "identify a research opportunity," but how do you find something—the **gap**—that doesn't even exist yet? You've got a column on **limitations & gaps** in your literature review database but how does one assimilate that to point out what's the gap?

The gap isn't empty space; it's **intellectual tension**. A PhD contribution rarely involves inventing something entirely new out of thin air. It involves bringing existing ideas, methods, or data together in a novel way to solve a problem that the current literature acknowledges but hasn't resolved.

Categories of research gaps

To help structure your critique, it is essential to categorize the type of deficiency you identify. A strong dissertation addresses a gap that can be clearly defined.

- **Evidence gap:** Conflicting or contradictory results exist in the current literature, and no research has synthesized or definitively resolved the debate on a topic.

- **Knowledge gap:** A lack of research or information exists on a particular topic that is foundational to the field. This is the most common and broadest category.

- **Practical knowledge gap:** Theory is well-established, but it doesn't translate or apply to real-world, practical contexts (e.g., a lab model fails in an industrial setting).

- **Methodological gap:** Existing research methods are outdated, limited in scope, or inappropriate for addressing the contemporary research question (e.g., requiring a new statistical model or data collection technique).

- **Empirical gap:** A lack of real-world, primary data is available to test or validate existing theories, or the existing data is flawed or insufficient.

- **Theoretical gap:** The clear conceptual framework or explanatory theory needed to explain a phenomenon is missing, insufficient, or inadequately developed.

- **Population gap:** Specific groups (e.g., cultural, demographic, geographic) have been ignored or excluded in previous studies, meaning existing findings cannot be generalized to them.

How to find one of these non-existent gap?

The key is to leverage the structured data in your **limitations & gaps** column of your database and there are couple different ways to go about this.

Look for tension (the "But")

Read the core contribution of paper A, then read the limitation of paper B. The gap is often the space between them.

Example: **paper A contribution:** we proved that model x is highly accurate for predicting housing prices in dense urban areas. **Paper B limitation:** model x fails entirely when applied to rural areas with low transaction volume.

Your gap: Develop a hybrid model that maintains model x's performance in urban areas **but** integrates a spatial-temporal component to make it viable for rural, low-data environments.

Look for methodological misalignment

If all the papers you read use method A, but new data (data B) is now available, the gap is applying the old method (A) to the new data (B), or creating a new method (C) to leverage data (B).

Look for consensus fatigue

If every paper agrees on a foundational premise, and you can find external evidence (from a different field, or recent societal change) that challenges that premise, you have found a massive theoretical gap.

Very often, the gap is not a ground breaking invention; it is a dissertation born from structured critique. It is the place where the current scholarly conversation has naturally paused, and your dissertation is the next required step in that conversation.

The dynamic database and the critical reading habits we've established turn the dreaded literature review from a reading task into a strategic project management task. You are now equipped to navigate the sea of papers with purpose, knowing exactly when to drop anchor and start building your own structure.

The next, and most crucial, step is to transform this carefully synthesized database into the single, guiding artifact of your entire PhD journey. The true value of your "limitations & gaps" column is not just critique, but **clarity of purpose**. This process is too vital to be reduced to simple writing techniques. In **Chapter 16: The masterful research question**, we will tackle the high-gamut task of assimilating the entire literature review database to definitively **carve out the research gap** and forge the **masterful research question** that will serve as the unshakable foundation of your entire dissertation. This question is the intellectual contract between you, your supervisor, and your field. This is what you need when someone asks you *"What's your PhD about?"*

16

The masterful research question

You have completed the difficult task of establishing a **dynamic literature review database** (Chapter 15) to plan and manage your literature review. You moved past passive reading and started actively hunting for the intellectual tension in your field—the **gaps**. This chapter provides the strategic compass for the highest-leverage task in your PhD: transforming the raw data of critique (your database) into the single, most important artifact of your candidature—your **masterful research question**. This question is your contract with the academic community; it determines your experiments, your chapters, and your legacy.

Strategy: Top-down vs. bottom-up approach

Before translating your database to a fundamental research question to guide your dissertation, it's essential to understand the two main philosophical approaches to carving out a research question. Most successful projects use a blend of both, but knowing your starting point can simplify the initial selection process.

The top-down (Deductive) approach

This approach starts with a **grand problem** or a large theoretical debate and narrows down to a manageable dissertation question.

- **Process:** Start with a broad, real-world issue (e.g., *How can AI be made socially responsible?*) and use the literature to find specific, unresolved facets within that domain.

- **Best for:** Students in highly theoretical, policy-driven, or paradigm-shifting fields (e.g., Philosophy, Ethics, Advanced Physics, Sociological Theory).

Pros: The resulting question is often highly significant and immediately addresses a major societal or scientific concern.

Cons: High risk of **scope creep**. It's easy to get lost in the bigness of the problem, and you might spend too much time defending the *problem* rather than solving your small, specific part of it.

The bottom-up (Inductive) approach

This approach starts with the **empirical data** and the **methodological gaps** found in your literature review and builds outwards to a broader claim.

- **Process:** Start with the specific failings in your "Limitations & Gaps" column (e.g., *All current models fail on longitudinal data sets*). The research question then asks how to resolve this specific, localized failure.
- **Best for:** Students in empirical, computational, or applied science fields (e.g., Engineering, Computer Science, Biology, Experimental Psychology).

Pros: The resulting question is immediately **doable** and has clear, measurable outcomes. You minimize scope creep because the question is anchored to a known methodological challenge.

Cons: The resulting question can sometimes be perceived as too narrow or a mere technical fix, requiring more effort in the writing phase to elevate its theoretical significance.

Recommendation: For most PhDs, the **bottom-up** approach, leveraging the gaps you already documented, is safer, faster, and reduces the risk of an unresolvable dissertation but at times, a hybrid approach may be desirable.

Now, the step-by-step guide to go from a list of papers you've read and added to your database to a strategic research question that is credible of a PhD dissertation will be done in multiple phases as follows:

Phase 1: From database critique to candidate questions

Your goal in this phase is to produce **3 to 5 candidate research questions (CRQs)**. Do not aim for perfection; aim for volume and variety.

Step 1: Cluster the gaps

Go to your database and filter/sort by the **Limitations & Gaps** column. You should see themes emerging. Cluster the papers based on *why* they failed or what they *didn't* address. For example:

- **Data cluster:** "Fails for high-dimensional data." "Only tested on synthetic data."
- **Methodology cluster:** "Black box, no interpretability." "Computationally too expensive for real-time use."
- **Scope cluster:** "Only tested in Western populations." "No long-term follow-up."

Step 2: Formulate the "Resolution Hypothesis"

For each of your 3–5 major clusters, draft a brief statement (1-2 sentences) on how you believe this specific gap can be resolved. This is your **Resolution Hypothesis**.

- *Data cluster resolution:* "The data complexity gap can be resolved by using a novel feature selection ensemble that prioritizes stability over absolute correlation."
- *Methodology cluster resolution:* "The computational expense can be reduced by approximating the core function with a parallelized heuristic algorithm."

Step 3: Convert the hypothesis into a question

Finally, convert each Resolution Hypothesis into a formal, concise, and focused research question. This shift from statement to question is critical, moving your assertion into a researchable inquiry.

- **From "Resolve by using a stable feature selection ensemble"** you get **CRQ 1:** How can an interpretable, stable feature selection ensemble enhance predictive performance in high-dimensional, noisy data streams?

- **From "Reduce computational expense via a parallelized heuristic approximation"** you get **CRQ 2:** What is the optimal parallelized heuristic approach to approximate Model X's core function while maintaining >95% prediction accuracy?

- **From "Generalize the findings to different geographical or demographic contexts"** you get **CRQ 3:** How do the policy implications of Model Y change when validated against non-Western, low-data populations, and what modifications are necessary for robust generalization?

Phase 2: Quantifying viability (The FIT Score)

You now have 3 to 5 exciting ideas. The danger is choosing the **most exciting** instead of the **most viable**. You must quantitatively score your CRQs based on three objective metrics that dictate PhD success. Use this simple **FIT Score** system (scored 1 to 5, where 5 is best).

The FIT score components

1. **Feasibility (F):** *Can I actually do this in 3-4 years?* Is the required data available (or collectable)? Do I have (or can I learn) the necessary technical skills (e.g., specific programming, lab work, rare equipment)? Is the required computational power accessible? A CRQ requiring an unreleased dataset or a new invention scores low (1-2).

2. **Impact (I):** *Who cares, and why is this novel?* Does this question resolve a key tension noted in your database? Does it lead to at least 3–4 distinct publications? Does it contribute a novel method, data set, or theoretical perspective? A CRQ that creates a new tool or resolves a long-standing methodological paradox scores high (4-5).

3. **Traction (T):** *Will my supervisor support this, and does it align with their current funding/interests?* Does this

question directly follow a conversation you've had with your advisor? Does it leverage skills or resources they already possess? This is crucial for job security and resources. A CRQ that is a logical extension of your advisor's current work scores high (4-5).

Scoring and selection

Total the scores for each CRQ (maximum score is 15).

- **Total Score 12-15:** Highly viable. Proceed to pitch this as your primary topic.
- **Total Score 8-11:** Potentially viable. Requires careful discussion with your advisor about the lowest-scoring component (usually Feasibility).
- **Total Score** 7 **or below:** High risk. Relegate this to a "Plan C" or discard it. The risk of stalling is too high.

Phase 3: Pitching and scoping for the pivot

The pitch to your advisor is not an academic debate; it is a **project management proposal**.

How to pitch your topic

1. **Present a primary and a plan B:** Present your highest-scoring CRQ (the "Primary") and one high-scoring alternative (the "Plan B").

2. **Focus on the gap, not the question:** Start the conversation by showing the **evidence** from your database. For instance: *"Professor, my literature review revealed a major tension: seven recent papers all conclude their models fail when scaled to multi-site deployment. They explicitly flag this as the critical barrier to real-world application."*

3. **Introduce the Master CRQ:** Only once the gap is established, introduce your proposed solution (the Primary CRQ) as the necessary next step to resolve that tension.

4. **Address the FIT score:** Proactively address the Feasibility component. *"I've checked the Feasibility, and I believe we can start this using the X dataset, which is publicly available, and I have already begun developing the required Y skill."*

Once you and your advisor reach a consensus, you have honed in on a prospective dissertation scope guided by your masterful research question with a high FIT score. But there is one more fail safe to be prepared for- the pivot.

The necessity of the pivot strategy

The moment you choose a research question, you are betting your dissertation on several core assumptions: that the data is cleanable and obtainable, the method is technically feasible, and the result will be non-trivial. The messy reality of research dictates that one of these assumptions may fail. If every thing falls apart, you don't want to go back to square one so it helps to be prepared with a pivot (your pre-meditated Plan B ready to deploy) to keep the momentum but not every pivot is viable and here is how to make this a structure strategy.

Pivot rule for your viable Plan B

Your Plan B CRQ should leverage the **same literature review database** and ideally, the **same core dataset or skills** as your Primary CRQ. If, six months in, you realize CRQ 1 is unfeasible (e.g., the primary dataset is junk), you pivot to CRQ 2. Because both questions emerged from the same cluster of gaps and the same synthesis, you lose minimal time. You simply use your existing resources to answer a related, but different, novel question. **Your supervisor will appreciate the foresight of having a viable Plan B ready.**

> *Having a Plan B ready doesn't mean you lack commitment to your primary plan, it just means you are prepared to safeguard the progress of your PhD dissertation at any cost to make it to the finish line.*
> *- Dr. Kshitij Tiwari*

You have now engineered your research question. It is specific, defensible, novel, and tied directly to the limitations acknowledged by your field. This question—your intellectual contract—provides the '**Why**' and the '**What**' of your PhD.

However, a superb question is useless without a surgical

plan of attack. You cannot start coding or running experiments without first establishing a clear, multi-year guide with quantifiable milestones. The next critical step is to translate this elegant masterful research question into a defined approach. In **Chapter 17: Selecting your methodological framework**, we will define the core research tradition (Qualitative, Quantitative, or Mixed-Methods) that will guide all subsequent design choices, moving us from the 'What' to the crucial 'How' of your research.

17

Selecting your methodological framework

Having formulated your **masterful research question** in the previous chapter, you must now answer a fundamental philosophical question: *How will knowledge be generated and evaluated within this dissertation?* The answer to this question guides every decision that follows, from the data collected to the types of conclusions that can be drawn.

This chapter details the three major methodological frameworks available to you, providing the necessary context for the detailed design work in subsequent chapters.

The quantitative framework

The quantitative framework is concerned with objective measurements and statistical analysis of data. It operates on the premise that reality is observable, measurable, and generalizable.

Key characteristics:

- **Purpose:** To test hypotheses, examine cause-and-effect relationships, and make predictions.
- **Data:** Numerical data (surveys, controlled experiments, existing datasets).
- **Analysis:** Statistical tests (e.g., ANOVA, regression, t-tests).
- **Outcome:** Findings are often generalizable to a larger population. This approach directly leads to the creation of **testable hypotheses**.

The qualitative framework

The qualitative framework seeks to understand the deeper context, meaning, and experiences of individuals or groups. It operates on the premise that reality is socially constructed and subjective.

Key characteristics:

- **Purpose:** To explore, describe, and understand complexity; to generate theory rather than test it.
- **Data:** Non-numerical data (interviews, focus groups, field observations, textual analysis).
- **Analysis:** Thematic analysis, discourse analysis, content analysis.

- **Outcome:** Rich, descriptive insights that provide a deep understanding of phenomena. This approach typically uses **research questions** and propositions instead of statistical hypotheses.

The mixed-methods framework

The mixed-methods framework combines both quantitative and qualitative approaches in a single study. This approach recognizes that neither framework alone is sufficient to fully capture the complexity of the research problem.

Key characteristics:

- **Purpose:** To achieve greater depth and breadth of understanding by triangulating findings.
- **Design:** Requires careful sequencing and integration of data (e.g., collecting qualitative data first to inform a quantitative survey, or vice-versa).
- **Outcome:** A comprehensive picture where numerical and descriptive findings reinforce or challenge each other. When using this framework, scholars often utilize **testable hypotheses** for the quantitative component and research questions for the qualitative component.

Each of these frameworks has their purpose and strengths so you must wondering- How does one pick among them?

When to choose which framework

The decision of which framework to use should be driven entirely by the nature of your Masterful Research Question and the desired outcome.

Quantitative is best when:

- You are building upon an established body of literature that already defines the key variables.
- Your goal is to confirm or refute a specific theoretical relationship using statistical rigor.
- You need to generalize findings to a larger population (answering questions like: "Does X predict Y?" or "What is the difference between group A and group B?", where statistical significance is key).

Qualitative is best when:

- Your topic is under-researched, and you need to explore and generate new theories or models.
- You seek a deep, nuanced understanding of a specific context or individual experience.
- The research relies on subjective data like feelings, opinions, or cultural context (answering questions like: "How do participants experience Z?" or "What are the underlying reasons for phenomenon P?" where rich detail is key).

Mixed-method is best when:

- The complexity of the problem requires both numerical validation and deep contextual explanation.
- You want one data type to validate or build upon the results of the other (e.g., using quantitative survey results to select participants for follow-up qualitative interviews). This framework helps explain the *extent* of a phenomenon and the *mechanism* behind it simultaneously.

The selection of one of these three frameworks—quantitative, qualitative, or mixed-methods—is the single most important strategic choice in your dissertation design. Having defined the fundamental philosophical approach of your research, we must now integrate this choice into the overall sequence and structure of your entire doctoral project. We turn next to **Chapter 18: The PhD dissertation framework**.

18

The PhD dissertation framework

You've successfully engineered your **masterful research question**. It is specific, defensible, and anchored to an established gap in the literature. Now, it's time to move from intellectual inquiry to **strategic project management**- your **dissertation framework**.

However, a single, comprehensive masterful research question cannot be answered in one monolithic effort. Instead, it must be strategically decomposed into several **Specific Aims** or **sub-questions**. Successfully managing these sub-questions requires you to treat your PhD not as a single long document, but as a **portfolio of smaller, sequential projects** that must be executed and published strategically.

This chapter provides a robust, customizable structure to transform your Masterful Question and its sub-questions into a multi-year execution plan, complete with quantifiable milestones for tracking progress.

The core dissertation structure: The 1-2-1 model

Your PhD dissertation is not a collection of loosely related papers; it is a single, cohesive, long-form argument proving that you are a master of independent research. Every chapter must build toward answering your **Masterful Research Question**. Regardless of your discipline—be it lab-based science, historical analysis, or computational modeling—most successful dissertations adhere to a flexible four-part structure.

The structure breaks down as follows:

- **The First '1' (Context):** A single, integrated section that sets up the problem.
- **The '2' (Core research):** Two distinct, substantial research projects that form the core of your novel contribution. **N.B.** There may be scenarios where you would need to expand to 3-5 projects though management becomes equally harder so balance this trade-off well in consultation with your supervisor.
- **The Final '1' (Synthesis):** A single, comprehensive chapter that ties the work together.

Understanding this structure is essential because your timeline exists only to produce these four parts:

1. **Part 1: The Context.** This encompasses the literature review, problem framing, and methodology. This

section establishes the why your research is necessary and the how you plan to execute it. In a standard timeline, this is the primary focus of Year 1.

2. **Part 2: Research Project A.** This is your first major data collection, experiment, or analysis block. It represents the first substantial novel contribution and often forms your first major publication. This is the primary focus of Year 2.

3. **Part 3: Research Project B.** This is your second distinct body of work. It may be an entirely new line of investigation or a critical extension of Project A (e.g., validating the model from A on a new dataset). This usually forms your second major publication and is the primary focus of Year 3.

4. **Part 4: Synthesis**. This includes the integrated discussion, conclusion, and future work. This section is where you connect the findings of Projects A and B back to the initial context and the Masterful Research Question. This is the dedicated focus of the final year.

But, these are anticipated time frames and life happens. There will be hurdles that will push back the timelines and unexpected delays stemming from uncontrolled factors. This is why you need a buffer.

Timeline strategy: Matching effort to duration

The key to a successful execution of a PhD framework is acknowledging the necessary buffer for failure, revisions, and unexpected delays. While a 3-year track is possible, it is intensely aggressive and leaves no margin for error. The 4 to 5-year track is highly recommended for maximizing publication output and minimizing stress.

The 3-Year (aggressive) schema

This track is primarily for students with pre-existing expertise or a highly focused, data-rich project (e.g., specific quantitative work). It demands absolute focus and often requires pre-emptive publication efforts.

1. ***Year 1***: Synthesis and Project A initiation. Your candidacy exam must be completed by month 6. You must finish the literature review and immediately launch into the first major experimental phase (Project A).

2. ***Year 2***: Execution and dual drafting. You complete Project A and submit your first publication while simultaneously beginning data collection and analysis for Project B. This is the most demanding period, combining execution and revision.

3. ***Year 3***: Final writing and submission. The research for Project B concludes by month 30. The remaining six

months are dedicated only to integrating the manuscript and submitting the final dissertation.

The 4-year (standard) schema

This is the standard model and is a disciplined but manageable pace, aligning perfectly with the 1-2-1 model.

1. ***Year 1***: Foundation and context. Secure ethics approvals, finish the literature review, pass the candidacy/transfer exam, and establish your core methodology pipeline. The goal is to start generating pilot data for Project A before the year ends.

2. ***Year 2***: Execution of Project A. Complete all data collection and analysis for Project A. Draft and submit your first major peer-reviewed journal or conference paper.

3. ***Year 3***: Execution of Project B. Pivot to Project B. Complete data collection and analysis, and submit your second major peer-reviewed paper. By the end of this year, all significant research should be completed.

4. ***Year 4***: Writing and integration. Dedicate the first six months to integrating Projects A and B into a cohesive manuscript. The final six months are for committee review, defense preparation, and submission.

The 5-year (strategic) schema

The most robust and recommended structure, offering a critical buffer. The added year is not time off; it is a year dedicated to maximizing the **impact** and **polish** of your work.

1. ***Years 1–3***: Follow the 4-year plan precisely. By the end of Year 3, you have completed the bulk of the research and submitted two papers.

2. ***Year 4***: The Buffer and high-impact year. This year is dedicated to addressing major revisions (revise and resubmit) on your submitted papers, conducting one smaller, high-impact follow-up experiment (Project C), or securing highly competitive external funding. This reduces submission stress and elevates your CV.

3. ***Year 5***: Dedicated writing and career transition. The entire year is focused exclusively on writing a highly polished dissertation manuscript, preparing for your defense, and applying for post-doctoral or industry positions.

Addressing extensions: The 6th and 7th year (exigent) strategy

If your program allows for, or, your circumstances necessitate a 6th or 7th year, the strategic focus must shift from **research completion** to **career maximization**.

- **Stop new research**: Unless absolutely necessary to answer a reviewer's comment on a major paper, stop all new experiments or data collection. The core dissertation is done.
- **Focus on major revisions**: Devote this time to getting your existing submitted papers accepted. A successful publication in a top journal is the highest-value activity you can perform.
- **Convert Chapters to review papers:** Take your polished literature review (Chapter 1) or your methodology chapter and transform it into a standalone review article for a reputable journal. Review articles are highly cited and demonstrate thought leadership, effectively turning one chapter into two publications.
- **Develop career artifacts**: Use the time to prepare teaching portfolios, secure small grants, or develop specialized skills (like advanced data visualization or a new statistical method). This reframes the extension as a period of professional development, not delay.

Quantifiable milestones for progress tracking

All the year-wise strategic schema are just theory without action if you cannot quantify your progress. You need granular, non-negotiable checkpoints to ensure momentum- **the milestones**. Break down your **Masterful research question** into these small, achievable steps.

Year 1: Foundation and scoping milestones

- By Month 3: Finalized, critiqued literature review database and a formal pivot plan (Chapter 10).
- By Month 6: Formal approval of your dissertation proposal/candidacy paper.
- By Month 9: Completed a Pilot Study, including the analysis pipeline (i.e., you can run your analysis code on dummy data).
- By Month 12: Draft of the Introduction and Methodology chapters (Part 1) submitted to your advisor for review.

Middle years: Execution and publishing milestones

- Quarterly: Complete a Core Experimental Block. This means all data for one specific experiment or analysis (e.g., "Simulation of Model X on Dataset A completed and results tabulated," or "Thematic analysis of 15 primary sources finalized").
- Bi-Annually: Submit a draft manuscript of a publication-ready paper (one in the Spring, one in the Fall) to your

advisor.

- Annually: Achieve at least one major external submission (journal or top-tier conference).
- Ongoing: Secure one presentation per year (department seminar, minor conference, or lab meeting).

Final years (the 6 month countdown): Writing and integration milestones

- 6 months before submission: The complete, integrated dissertation manuscript (all chapters including Discussion and Conclusion) is submitted to your advisor.
- 3 month before submission: All figures, tables, and references for the entire dissertation are finalized, captioned, and placed correctly.
- 1 month before submission: Final, proofread copy approved by the advisor and ready for formatting according to institutional rules.

The PhD is won in the planning phase. By breaking the intimidating task into these quantifiable units, and having fail safes even for your fail safes, you guarantee that every day's work moves you demonstrably toward your final defense.

However, a brilliant plan without funding is merely a wish. Before you can detail the specific hypotheses and experimental methods you will use, you must first prove that your timeline is **financially feasible**. This foresight is crucial for the committee.

The next step is to decide how you will pay for the fieldwork, software, travel, and specialized equipment laid out in your framework. In **Chapter 19: Financial architecture of**

research, we will detail the critical steps for budgeting, securing grants, and strategically allocating resources to ensure your research plan is not just smart, but **executable**.

19

Financial architecture of research

The pursuit of a PhD is fundamentally a financial enterprise, requiring not only intellectual capital but also sustained, strategic monetary resources. This chapter moves beyond your personal stipend to explore the broader financial architecture of research: how money is secured, budgeted, managed, and ethically reported within an institutional setting. Mastering this domain is crucial for success as a doctoral student and for planning your research trajectory- this is the fuel of your PhD dissertation framework.

The landscape of funding: Stipends and student roles

Understanding when and how a PhD scholar applies for funding requires recognizing the difference between securing personal support (a stipend) and securing project resources (a grant).

1. Is a secured stipend the norm? (System variation)

The expectation of a **secured stipend** (a salary to cover living expenses) is highly dependent on the academic system and discipline.

- **The North American model (US/Canada):** It is the **norm** to be **"fully funded"** for 4 to 6 years. The stipend is typically guaranteed upon admission and comes from a combination of **Teaching Assistantships (TAs)**, **Research Assistantships (RAs)** paid by the supervisor's grant (**PI Grant**), or University Fellowships. Students are generally *not* required to apply for their initial stipend.

- **The European model (UK, Australia, Continental Europe):** Securing funding is often a prerequisite for admission. Students are either recruited onto a specific, already-funded project (which includes a stipend) or they apply for competitive, national-level scholarships. In many parts of Continental Europe, the PhD is treated as a research job with a contract, ensuring a secure salary/stipend from the outset.

- **The Asia-Pacific model (Singapore, Hong Kong, Japan, China):** This model emphasizes highly centralized, **merit-based, fully-funded fellowships** provided directly by the government or top-tier universities themselves. Acceptance into a premier program often automatically includes a substantial, non-service-required stipend (i.e., no mandatory teaching or research assistantship duties in exchange for the funding), tuition waiver, and travel allowance. The focus is on attracting international talent and competitive excellence, where the funding acts as a powerful recruitment tool.

If you are accepted into a **"fully funded" PhD program**, your stipend is secure initially. If your program is *not* fully funded, securing your own stipend is usually mandatory for enrollment. **N.B.** This wasn't meant to be an exhaustive list of PhD admission and financial models but were more to show you that academia isn't a unified system around the globe. So, when you sign up for a PhD, especially PhD abroad, you must understand these nuances aside from evaluating the advisor-advisee fit for your PhD journey.

2. When does a PhD scholar apply for funding?

A PhD scholar needs to apply for funding not to pay for themselves (if they are fully funded), but primarily to pay for the **research itself**. This typically happens under three circumstances:

- **To cover specific research costs:** Even with a secure stipend, the PI Grant might not cover all your specific expenses. Students often apply for smaller, targeted grants starting in their second or third year for **direct costs** such as:

Fieldwork: *Trips to archives, remote data collection sites, or required facility use.*

Conference travel: *To present your work in later*

years, especially international travel.

Specialized supplies: *Unique software licenses, transcription services, or high* ***article***

processing charges *(APCs) for Open Access publication.*

- **To gain a competitive edge (The Fellowship Goal):** Applying for and winning a personal, competitive fellowship (e.g., a national or institutional award) is a crucial career distinction. It signals independence and competitive excellence to future employers.
- **When initial funding expires:** If institutional funding or the PI's grant runs out, the student must apply for grants or fellowships to cover the final year(s) of dissertation completion.

3. PI Grants vs. Student Fellowships: Roles and credit

There is a clear division of labor and credit:

- **Principal Investigator (PI) and Project Grants:** The PI (your supervisor) writes and manages large grants (e.g., federal science or humanities grants) that fund the **entire multi-year multi-personnel project**. These cover equipment, materials, and pay the stipends/salaries of the **Research Assistants (RAs)**—which includes PhD students. The PI receives the formal credit for securing the grant. In some cases, your PI may ask you to write some parts of the grant proposal too but at the end of they day, they will get the credit if the grant is secured.

- **The PhD Student and Personal Fellowships:** The student applies for **fellowships** or **trainee awards**. The student writes the application focused on their **personal research** and **career development** plan. The student receives the formal credit as the **Awardee** or **Fellow**, which is a highly valued achievement on their CV.

Strategic funding acquisition and grant anatomy

Mastering the mechanics of the grant application process is essential for the transition to a research-focused career.

1. Understanding the funding landscape

Research funding generally falls into three categories:

- **Government/Public funding:** Large, competitive grants provided by national bodies (e.g., NSF, ERC, UKRI). These often fund long-term projects (3–5 years) and require high-potential public benefit.
- **Foundation/Non-Profit funding:** Grants from private or charitable foundations (e.g., Gates Foundation, Wellcome Trust, field-specific societies). These are often narrower in scope and focused on specific societal or applied problems.
- **Institutional/Internal funding:** Smaller grants offered by your own university or department. These are crucial

for **pilot studies**, **travel to preliminary data collection sites**, or supporting research assistants for initial phases.

2. The core components of a research budget

The budget is the numerical translation of your research plan. It must be detailed, justified, and directly link every dollar requested to a specific methodological objective. Remember: these are **non-stipend** costs that must be covered by the grant.

A. Direct Costs

These are expenses directly attributable to the project and must be justified precisely:

- **Personnel:** Salaries and benefits for Research Assistants (RAs), Post-Doctoral Researchers, and Technicians. Justify the time commitment (e.g., "50% FTE for a Research Assistant for 12 months to conduct all 1,500 surveys").

- **Equipment:** Purchase or lease of major items (e.g., specialized instruments, high-performance computing clusters). Justify why existing institutional equipment cannot be used.

- **Supplies and materials:** Consumables (e.g., reagents, transcription services, **participant compensation**). Break down costs to the unit level (e.g., "500 culture plates @ $1.50 each"). **Avoid generic "Miscellaneous supplies."**

- **Travel:** Necessary trips for **data collection** (fieldwork), facility use, or **presenting initial findings** (conferences). Justify the necessity with specific details.

- **Publication fees:** Open Access (OA) article processing charges (APCs) and professional editing.

B. Indirect Costs (F&A - Facilities and administrative costs)

This is a fixed percentage (often 40% to 70%) applied to the Direct Costs. This money goes to the university to cover overhead like library subscriptions, utilities, and building maintenance. You must factor it into your total request, but you do not control its use.

3. Writing the budget justification narrative

The justification is the argumentative essay accompanying your budget form. Its purpose is to demonstrate value for money and feasibility.

- **Narrative clarity:** Ensure the narrative flows logically, moving line-by-line through the budget form.

- **The "Goldilocks" principle:** The budget should be not too big (appearing inefficient) and not too small (raising doubts about feasibility). Reviewers are highly attuned to unrealistically low budgets, which signal poor planning.

- **Contingency planning:** While dedicated "Contingency" line items are often disallowed, your justification should subtly account for common overruns (e.g., "Personnel costs include a 3% annual increase to account for institutional salary inflation").

Financial compliance and post-award management

Winning a grant is only the halfway point. Effective post-award management ensures the project stays within budget and meets reporting requirements.

1. Institutional financial systems and protocols

Once awarded, funding is managed through a central university system as the money doesn't get credited to your bank account directly. Your grant will be assigned a unique **Cost Centre or Project Code**.

- **Understanding procurement:** All spending must be processed through the university's procurement system. Learn the rules for expense limits, competitive bidding for large purchases, and approved vendors.

- **Record keeping:** Maintain a meticulous **audit trail** for every single expense: invoices, receipts, proof of delivery, and signed purchase orders. If the purchase cannot be traced back to the project, the expense will be rejected.

2. Time and effort reporting

This is one of the most critical aspects of compliance, especially for PIs who charge a portion of their salary to the grant.

- **The certification mandate:** Institutions require periodic certification that the effort expended on the grant (e.g., "50% effort") accurately reflects the work performed during that period.

- **Avoiding co-mingling:** You must be able to demonstrate that personnel time was dedicated to the specific grant for which they were paid, and not mixed with teaching or unrelated administrative duties.

3. Financial reporting to the funder

Every grant agreement includes a schedule for financial and scientific reporting- though the reporting frequency varies across funders.

- **Interim financial reports:** These detail the expenditures to date, the remaining balance, and any planned re-budgeting.

- **Re-budgeting:** If you need to shift funds between major categories (e.g., moving money from Travel to Supplies), you may require formal, written approval from the funding agency, guided by institutional research services.

- **Final report and closeout:** The closeout process requires meticulous final financial statements and documentation that the funds were spent entirely within the defined project period and scope.

The economics of the Doctoral journey

While the grant focuses on the project, the individual researcher must adopt a strategic financial mindset regarding their degree trajectory and future preparation.

1. Strategic fellowship and award applications

Early-career fellowships are financially significant and represent a massive career advantage for students.

- **Research Grants (PI Status):** While these are primarily managed by your supervisor, securing these funds establishes independence, trains personnel, and builds a track record of funding success.

- **Personal Fellowships (Post-Docs):** These often provide protected, non-teaching research time and demonstrate competitive excellence on an international stage, setting you up for highly sought-after future roles.

2. Leveraging the PhD stipend

View your PhD stipend (or scholarship) as an investment in human capital.

- **Minimize debt:** The stipend allows you to dedicate time fully to research and minimizes the need for external employment, which directly accelerates your degree completion time.

- **Build an emergency fund:** Given the precarious nature of early-career academic hiring, maintaining a robust savings cushion is crucial for flexibility and weathering job market uncertainties post-graduation.

3. The economics of publication

The current publication model has financial implications that must be planned for. The transition to Open Access (OA) publishing means researchers must budget for Article Processing Charges (APCs).

- **Planning for APCs:** Incorporate APC costs into every grant application. Relying solely on departmental funds can drain resources or delay publication.

- **Copyright and Licensing:** Understand the financial implications of different licensing models (e.g., CC BY vs. CC BY-NC) as they dictate who can reuse your work and under what terms.

Now that you have a better understanding of the funding landscape and the economics of a Doctoral journey, you must be wondering- When do you begin the funding paperwork? Let's understand more about when you switch gears from scrolling to applying for funding.

Strategic timing and the shifting landscape of opportunity awareness

While the principle of maintaining constant awareness of funding opportunities remains critical, the shift from *casual observation* to *active application* is a highly variable and strategic decision. Initially, a scholar should use opportunity scouting to inform their research direction, treating the process as a high-level survey of the competitive landscape- similar to a literature review but this time for the funding opportunities.

The tipping point for transitioning to active application usually aligns with the successful definition of core research questions, completion of necessary foundational coursework, or the formal designation of the scholar as an independent research candidate, as per institutional guidelines. At this stage, the opportunities sought move from general scholarships to those targeted specifically at dissertation execution, fieldwork, or specialized equipment acquisition.

Financial preparedness: From budgeting to formal planning

Similarly, the necessary depth of financial preparedness evolves. Early in the PhD journey, maintaining a responsible personal budget and understanding the cost of attendance is usually sufficient. However, upon transitioning to the status of a fully independent researcher—often when submitting a comprehensive research proposal or candidacy document—the requirements shift. At this stage, institutions frequently require a formalized financial plan.

This formalized planning involves more than just personal budgeting; it necessitates detailed projections of research costs (including consumables, travel, and publication fees), a structured grant strategy for targeted funding, and contingency budgeting to account for unforeseen expenses or delays. This increased level of detail serves as a critical professional exercise, demonstrating the scholar's readiness to manage the scope and resources of a multi-year research endeavor.

The successful management of external opportunities and the establishment of a robust financial framework do not exist in a vacuum; they provide the essential practical foundation for the research itself. The resource landscape—whether it involves secured grants, fellowship deadlines, or institutional budget constraints—directly dictates the *feasibility* and *scope* of the research questions that can be explored.

Understanding these resource constraints is the vital precursor to defining the research challenge. Therefore, having established the practical parameters of our journey, we must now pivot to defining the intellectual heart of the dissertation:

the testable propositions and the plan to investigate them. This leads us directly to the framework we will explore in the next chapter.

20

Hypotheses and the experimental blueprint

In **Chapter 19**, we established the crucial practical and financial boundaries of your research journey, ensuring that your masterful research question is grounded in reality and supported by a robust budget and grant strategy. With the feasibility and scope now defined by your resource landscape, the next critical step is to solidify the intellectual foundation of your work.

This chapter focuses on converting your central question into testable propositions (Hypotheses) and translating those into a detailed, operational plan—the Experimental Blueprint. We will define precisely what you are seeking and precisely how you will find it through operationalization and procedure.

The anatomy of a testable hypothesis

If your methodology is quantitative or mixed-methods, you must move beyond the broad research question and define one or more testable hypotheses. A hypothesis is a specific, informed prediction about the relationship between two or more variables. It must be specific enough to be supported or refuted by statistical analysis.

Null (H0) and alternative (HA) hypotheses

For statistical testing, you must define two opposing statements:

- **The null hypothesis (H0):** This is the statement of no effect or no difference. It assumes that any observed patterns in your data are due purely to chance. This is the statement you attempt to statistically disprove (reject).
- **The alternative hypothesis (HA or H1):** This is the statement that your research expects to support. It suggests that a real relationship or difference exists between the variables.

Qualitative propositions and aims

For purely qualitative studies, you generally do not use formal null hypotheses. Instead, you focus on research aims or propositions that guide your exploration without making a fixed prediction. These are framed as statements of inquiry.

Operationalization: From concept to measurement

Many concepts we study in academia—such as resilience, expertise, or quality of life—are abstract constructs. To study them empirically, you must define them in a way that makes them measurable. This is the process of operationalization.

Defining variables

A successful research blueprint clearly defines how each abstract construct will be turned into a concrete, measurable variable:

- **Identify the construct:** The abstract concept (e.g., Procrastination).
- **Define the dimensions:** The components of the construct (e.g., Task delay, Avoidance behavior, Time mismanagement).
- **Select the indicator (Operational definition):** The specific, quantifiable way you will capture the dimension.
- **Quantitative indicator example:** The total score on the

Procrastination Assessment Scale for Students (PASS), a validated 20-item instrument.
- **Qualitative indicator example:** The frequency and depth of thematic mentions of "delaying work" or "feeling paralyzed" within semi-structured interview transcripts.

Measurement scales (Quantitative studies)

Operationalization also requires specifying the type of data your variable will yield, as this dictates the appropriate statistical analysis (Chapter 17).

- **Nominal:** Categories only (e.g., Gender: Male, Female, Non-binary).
- **Ordinal:** Categories with a rank order (e.g., Education level: High School, Bachelor's, Master's).
- **Interval:** Ordered, equal intervals, but no true zero (e.g., Temperature in Celsius).
- **Ratio:** Ordered, equal intervals, with a true zero (e.g., Age, Income, Time to completion).

The experimental blueprint: Your procedural manual

This blueprint is the most practical component of your methodology chapter. It is a precise, step-by-step guide to execution, which reviewers will scrutinize for feasibility and rigor.

- **Sampling strategy:** You must justify who you are collecting data from and why that sample is appropriate for your research question. Justify the final sample size using **Power Analysis** (quantitative) or the concept of **Saturation** (qualitative).

- **Instrumentation and ethics:** Detail every tool you will use for data collection. State if you are using **Validated Instruments** and the established reliability ($\alpha = 0.88$). Include key questions for **Interview/Focus Group Protocols**. State that your procedure has been approved by your institution's **Institutional Review Board (IRB)** or Ethics Committee.

- **The step-by-step protocol:** This is the timeline and procedure. Detail the **recruitment** method, the sequence of the **Data Collection** events, and how and where the raw data is **securely stored** (e.g., encrypted server, password protection).

With your hypotheses defined, your variables operationalized, and your protocol meticulously detailed, your methodological plan is complete. You have successfully mapped the journey from abstract idea to empirical measurement.

This detailed blueprint forms the core of your defense document. The next step is the formal academic test of your plan. **Chapter 21: The PhD candidacy and proposal defense** will guide you through packaging this blueprint into a robust proposal, navigating the committee review, and formally achieving candidacy status.

21

The PhD candidacy and proposal defense

The doctoral journey is punctuated by several formal defense milestones, and their names and structures vary widely by institution and country. For an early-stage scholar, understanding the subtle yet crucial differences between a Proposal Defense, a Candidacy Exam, and a Pre-Defense is essential for managing anxiety and preparing correctly.

This chapter focuses on the Candidacy and Proposal Defense—the first official defense of your detailed research plan. It is the moment you transition from being a doctoral student to an approved doctoral candidate. This chapter also explains how to curate a balanced committee as they will be an integral part of your journey from hereon and hold the key to your success on final defense day.

Decoding the defense milestones

The terminology can be confusing because universities often merge or rename these steps. Here is the core distinction you must internalize:

- **Qualifying or comprehensive exam (The knowledge check):** This is often a written or oral exam that tests your mastery of the entire field, usually occurring at the end of Year 2. Passing this proves you have the required knowledge depth.

- **Proposal defense (The plan check):** This is the focus of this chapter. It is the formal defense of your specific dissertation plan (your framework, budget, and blueprint). Your committee scrutinizes the feasibility and originality of your approach. This is often the final step required for Advancement to Candidacy.

- **Pre-defense or mock defense (The rehearsal):** If offered, this is an internal, non-binding practice run, typically held 3–6 months before the final defense to catch major flaws. It prepares you for the intellectual rigor of the final event.

- **Final defense or viva voce (The culmination):** This is the defense of the completed dissertation (covered later in the book). It is the final examination on your contribution and is distinct from the defense of your plan.

Curating your committee: Choosing your border guards

In most programs, you have a say in who sits on your committee. Do not leave this decision solely to your supervisor. You need a balanced panel that provides a **360-degree stress test** of your proposal.

The ideal committee composition:

- **The Methodologist:** Someone who is an expert in your specific research design (e.g., a statistician or a qualitative expert). Their role is to ensure your "how" is unshakeable.

- **The Subject Matter Expert (SME):** A scholar deeply embedded in your specific niche. They will ensure your "what" is truly novel and hasn't been done before.

- **The "Devil's Advocate":** A faculty member known for asking tough, foundational questions. While intimidating, having them on your proposal committee prevents surprises at your final defense.

- **The Supportive Generalist:** A senior faculty member who understands the broader institutional requirements and can act as a stabilizing force if the subject matter experts disagree.

Strategic Tip: Before inviting someone to your committee, look at their recent publications and, if possible, attend a defense where they are a member. Observe their questioning style. You are looking for "rigorous but fair," not "adversarial for the sake of ego." Also, some programs may have a mandate for the composition of the committee to balance the internal and external committee member participation. Make sure to check for any such requirements with your advisor before you start doing outreach to invite committee members. After all, you don't want to do all the outreach effort, onboard a member and then have to offboard them immediately because the Committee composition does not follow the mandates of your program.

The anatomy of a winning proposal document

Before you stand in front of a committee, you must produce a document that serves as your **intellectual blueprint**. A successful proposal is not a "mini-thesis"; it is a justification of future work. It must contain:

1. **The problem statement:** A crisp, high-urgency definition of the gap you are filling.
2. **The masterful research question:** The central pivot point of the entire document.
3. **Literature synthesis:** Not just a list of what others did, but a narrative that leads the reader to the inevitable conclusion that *your* study is the next logical step.
4. **Methodological justification:** A rigorous defense of why your chosen methods are the most appropriate tools

for the job.

5. **Pilot data (If available):** Brief evidence that your proposed methods are feasible and that you possess the technical skill to execute them. If pilot data isn't already available, then you can pitch a plan on pilot data acquisition- be it yourself or in collaboration with others.
6. **Timeline and resource plan:** A realistic schedule proving the project can be completed within the remaining years of your degree.

Building your methodological justification

Your goal in the proposal defense is to preemptively defend your methodological choices against expert scrutiny. The methodology chapter of your proposal must follow this logical structure:

- **State your epistemology/ontology:** Briefly define your philosophical stance (e.g., "this research adopts a critical realist perspective... justifying a mixed-methods design.")

- **Link question to method:** Explain why your Research Question *requires* the chosen approach.

- **Specify the design:** Clearly state which specific design (e.g., explanatory sequential) you are using.

- **Acknowledge limitations:** Don't wait for the committee to find the flaws. State them upfront. This demonstrates intellectual maturity.

The Q&A: Handling the committee's scrutiny

The oral defense is where many students freeze. The committee is not there to "catch" you; they are there to stress-test your plan so you don't fail later during data collection.

The Strategy of Professional Defense:

- **The "Pause and Validate" Technique:** When asked a difficult question, don't rush to answer. Pause, say "That is an interesting perspective on the methodology," and take three seconds to frame your response.

- **Defensive Alignment:** If a committee member suggests a different method, explain *why* you chose your current path first. Show openness to their expertise, but demonstrate that your choice was intentional, not accidental.

- **Admit the Unknown:** If you are asked something truly outside your scope, it is okay to say: "That is outside the current scope of this proposal, but it is a compelling direction for future work post-candidacy."

The Candidacy Readiness Audit

To ensure the day of the proposal defense runs smoothly and focuses only on your ideas (not technical failures), run through this audit 24 hours prior:

- **The Visual Logic Check:** Do your slides exactly match the core arguments in your written proposal? Ensure no new data or contradictory claims appear on the screen.
- **The Technical Redundancy:** Have your presentation saved on a cloud drive, a physical USB, and the local hard drive of the laptop you are using.
- **The Administrative Paperwork:** Ensure all candidacy forms, ethics approval letters (IRB), and supervisor signature pages are printed and ready.

Navigating the outcome: "Pass with Revisions"

The most common outcome of a proposal defense is a **Pass with revisions**. Many students interpret this as a failure, but it is actually a vital part of the academic vetting process.

The committee's job is to strengthen your plan. If they ask for a larger sample size or a different statistical test, they are protecting you from reaching your final defense with a flawed dissertation. Treat these revisions as a **mandatory strategy update**. Once you integrate these changes, your "intellectual contract" is signed, and you are officially a

Doctoral Candidate.

You have established the "why" (your question) and the "how" (your method). With the core research plan now secure and formally approved, the next strategic step is to maximize your professional leverage. **Chapter 22: Strategic work experience via internship** will focus on how to use your candidacy status to pursue external professional immersion and build career skills before starting full-scale data collection.

22

Strategic work experience via internship

The previous chapter detailed the **PhD candidacy and proposal defense**—the pivotal moment when you establish yourself as an independent scholar with a defensible plan in front of your Committee. This milestone signifies the end of the preparation phase and the beginning of the research execution phase. You have clarity, a timeline, and, crucially, a stable platform.

This stability is your most valuable asset when considering a strategic professional immersion, most commonly in the form of a **PhD internship**. In the modern academic landscape, the internship is no longer an optional side-quest; it is a critical opportunity to build professional skills, diversify your network, and test potential career paths outside of academia before you invest years in the final dissertation effort.

The strategic value of mid-program immersion

A PhD internship should be strategically placed after the proposal defense for several key reasons:

1. **Gained leverage:** Post-defense, you are a credible scholar. You have proven you can formulate an independent research project, which makes you a more valuable asset to external organizations.

2. **Reduced risk:** By stabilizing your research plan, you minimize the risk that a temporary absence will derail your progress. The internship can be planned during a natural pause, such as between data collection phases or before a major writing push.

3. **Career testing:** For the vast majority of PhDs who transition to industry, policy, or non-profit roles, an internship provides necessary, real-world context. It allows you to confirm a career interest or, just as importantly, rule one out without committing to a full-time job after graduation.

4. **Future collaborations & career transition**: You never know what the future holds in store for you. There is always a chance that you enjoy your internship so much and excel at the tasks that you may be given a standing offer to join full-time after your final PhD defense. Or, you may end up establishing a direct line of communication for future collaborations and collaborations are the backbone for your PhD journey.

Navigating the internship landscape

PhD internships generally fall into two categories, and your choice should align with your long-term goals:

- **Industry/Policy internships:** These focus on transferring your foundational skills (data analysis, critical thinking, complex problem-solving) into a non-academic setting. The value here is in mastering **translating** academic insights into organizational impact and corporate strategy.

- **Research-aligned fellowships:** These allow you to work at a different university, national lab, or research institution, often building a specialized methodology or leveraging equipment your home institution lacks. The value is direct skill enhancement and widening your academic collaborations.

The supervisor conversation

A successful internship is always a tripartite negotiation involving you, your PhD advisor (supervisor), and the external organization. Transparency and early communication are paramount.

Approach your supervisor with a clear, well-researched proposal that details:

1. **The timeframe:** The exact start and end dates.
2. **The benefit:** How the internship experience (e.g., learning a new coding language, analyzing massive datasets, understanding policy formulation) will ultimately *strengthen* your dissertation or your career prospects.
3. **Contingency planning:** How you will manage your existing doctoral duties or cover any unexpected events during your absence.

Frame the internship not as a distraction, but as a **professional development tool** that will make you a more competitive and capable scholar upon your return. This strategic immersion will broaden your perspective and enhance your skills, ensuring that the work you perform in the next critical phase—**Execution and data management**—is informed by real-world relevance.

23

Execution and data management

Having completed your strategic professional immersion, you return to your doctoral project with a refreshed perspective and potentially advanced organizational skills acquired in an external setting. This transition—from a state of external professional development back to the core, meticulously planned blueprint of your dissertation—marks the shift into active data collection, often the most demanding part of the PhD journey.

This phase requires discipline, meticulous organizational skills, and strict adherence to ethical and methodological standards. The goal of execution is not just to gather data, but to gather high-quality, trustworthy data that can withstand rigorous scrutiny. This chapter provides the tactical guide for launching your study, ensuring ethical compliance, and establishing robust systems for data integrity, applying the professional rigor you've recently cultivated.

Pre-launch phase: The pilot study

Never assume your instruments or protocols will work perfectly the first time. The **pilot study** is your low stakes dry run, designed to iron out any procedural flaws before you commit resources (time, money, participants) to the main study.

The purpose of piloting

A pilot study should be a small-scale simulation of your main study, involving a few participants who resemble your target sample. Its key objectives are to:

- **Test instruments:** Check for clarity and ambiguity in survey questions, interview prompts, or experimental tasks. Do participants interpret the items as intended?

- **Time procedures:** Accurately gauge how long the experiment or interview takes. Unexpected duration can lead to participant fatigue or drop-out.

- **Validate analysis tools:** Test your data recording systems, software, and proposed analytical methods. Ensure the data comes out in a usable format.

- **Recruitment strategy:** Test the feasibility and efficiency of your chosen recruitment method.

Refining your protocol

After the pilot, you **must** document all necessary changes to your procedure, instruments, and even your sample size justification. If any changes significantly alter the ethical risk, they must be reported to your **Institutional Review Board (IRB)** for approval before the main launch.

The foundational requirement: The Data Management Plan (DMP)

Before commencing data collection, your final pre-launch artifact must be a formal **Data Management Plan (DMP)**. This document serves as a proactive, living strategy for the entire data lifecycle, from collection and storage through preservation and eventual disposal. Many funding bodies and Institutional Review Boards (IRBs) now require a DMP as a mandatory component of ethical approval.

A well-crafted DMP is essential because it guarantees that your commitment to data integrity and security is pre-planned, auditable, and repeatable.

Core components of a DMP:

- **Data description:** Detailed information on the type of data collected (e.g., quantitative, qualitative, experimental), its volume, and its technical format.

- **Security and storage:** The specific technical measures (e.g., encryption, restricted access, server location) you will use to protect data during the active research phase.

- **Roles and responsibilities:** Clearly identifying who is responsible for data cleaning, security, archiving, and responding to data access requests.

- **Data sharing and access:** Defining when, how, and to whom the anonymized or aggregated data will be made available after the project concludes (e.g., deposited in a public repository).

- **Data preservation and retention:** The timeline for how long the raw data will be kept after publication (often 5 to 10 years per institutional policy) and the long-term archiving solution used.

While the DMP critically outlines the data lifecycle, another aspect to be addressed before executing the data collection is ethical consideration.

Ethical execution: Compliance and consent

Ethical rigor is the bedrock of credible research. Violations—even accidental ones—can invalidate your entire project.

Informed consent in practice

Informed consent is an ongoing process, not a signed piece of paper. You must ensure that participants:

- **Comprehend the study:** Clearly understand the purpose, procedures, risks, and benefits in accessible language.
- **Understand voluntariness:** Know they can withdraw at any point, without penalty, even after the study has started.
- **Anonymity vs. confidentiality:** Clearly explain the distinction. **Anonymity:** Data cannot be linked to the individual (e.g., anonymous online survey). **Confidentiality:** Researcher knows the identity but protects it fiercely (e.g., pseudonymizing interview transcripts). *Always* promise confidentiality unless anonymity is guaranteed.

Data security compliance

Know and comply with the data protection regulations relevant to your region and field (e.g., **GDPR** in Europe, **HIPAA** for health data in the US). This involves using:

- **Secure storage:** Encrypted folders or approved institutional servers for storing raw data. **Never** store sensitive data on personal laptops or public cloud services without encryption.

- **De-identification:** Immediately separate identifying information (like names or contact details) from the research data and store them in two separate, secure locations.

Maintaining data integrity and fidelity

Integrity refers to the accuracy, completeness, and consistency of your data. Low integrity means low trust in your conclusions. Here is a suggested data management workflow:

1. Data organization and naming conventions

Establish a clear, consistent structure **before** collection begins.

- **Folder structure:** Create dedicated folders for: Raw Data (Read-Only), Cleaned Data, Analysis Scripts, Analysis Outputs, and Consent Forms (Separate).

- **File naming:** Use a systematic convention that includes the project, date, and version (e.g., PHD_SurveyData_20251029_v1.csv). **Never** rely on generic names like Data_Final.xlsx.

2. Data quality checks and cleaning

The cleaning process is often the most time-consuming step before analysis.

- **Missing data:** Identify patterns in missing data (e.g., if everyone skips question 10). Decide on a strategy: **Imputation** (estimating missing values) or **Exclusion**.

- **Outliers:** Identify values that fall far outside the expected range. Determine if they represent measurement error or a genuine, albeit rare, observation. Do not automatically remove outliers; decisions must be based on statistical justification and documented.

- **Data transformation:** Convert qualitative codes into numerical variables, aggregate items into composite scores, or standardize variables (e.g., calculating z-scores).

3. The audit trail

An **audit trail** is a log documenting every change made from the moment the data was collected to the final version used for analysis.

- **Log every action:** Record the date, the action taken (e.g., "Removed two participants due to incomplete consent," "Recoded gender variable to binary 0/1"), and the reasoning.

- **Protect raw data:** Your initial raw data file must be protected and never altered. All cleaning and manipulation must occur on a **copy**. This allows you to revert to the original if needed and prove the integrity of your process.

The execution phase is essentially a massive quality control operation. By prioritizing the ethical handling of participants and creating a rigorous, auditable data management system, you ensure that the hard work of analysis is built on a solid foundation.

With your data secured and cleaned, you are ready to put on your analyst hat and begin the final transformation of raw numbers and transcripts into meaningful insights. **Chapter 24: The art of data interrogation**, awaits.

24

The art of data interrogation

Following the successful execution of your research and the meticulous maintenance of data integrity, you now sit before the great mountain of raw information. This is the moment of truth. Data collection is the craft of your PhD; data interrogation is the science and the art.

This chapter guides you through the process of systematic analysis, showing you how to move beyond mere computation to discover the compelling narrative hidden within your dataset, ensuring your findings directly answer your Masterful Research Question.

The principle of methodological alignment

The method of interrogation must perfectly align with the methodological framework you defended in your proposal. You cannot use quantitative tools to interpret qualitative data, or vice versa. The process starts with preparing your data for the chosen approach.

Initial data preparation (All methods)

- **Data scrubbing**: This is the essential first step. Remove redundant entries, correct typographical errors, and standardize formats.
- **Missing data cleanup**: Decide how to handle missing data points (e.g., list-wise deletion, imputation) and document your reasoning.
- **Data security check**: Confirm all raw and processed files are stored securely and ethically, with personal identifiers removed or masked.

Interrogating quantitative data

Quantitative analysis is a structured process designed to test hypotheses and establish generalizable relationships using statistical tools.

The quantitative analysis process

- **Descriptive statistics**: Begin by summarizing your sample and variables (e.g., means, standard deviations, frequencies). This provides the essential context for your sample.

- **Assumptions testing**: Before running inferential tests, check if your data meets the statistical assumptions of the chosen test (e.g., normality, homogeneity of variance). Failure to do this invalidates your results.

- **Inferential statistics**: Run the specific tests (e.g., t-tests, ANOVA, regression) designed to test your null hypotheses (H0).

- **Interpretation**: Focus on two things: the **p-value** (does a statistically significant relationship exist?) and the **effect size** (how meaningful is the relationship?). A small effect size, even if significant, may not be theoretically important.

- **Visualization**: Create clean, clear charts and graphs (e.g., scatter plots, bar charts) to communicate your results effectively, ensuring they adhere to the conventions of your field.

Interrogating qualitative data

Qualitative analysis is an iterative, interpretive process focused on revealing themes, patterns, and meanings within text, audio, or visual data. It requires transparency and rigor to establish trustworthiness.

The qualitative analysis process

- **Transcription**: Convert all audio/video data into accurate text transcripts. This is a crucial foundation.

- **Coding**: Begin the process of labeling and classifying segments of your data (words, phrases, paragraphs) with short descriptive codes.

- **Thematizing**: Group related codes into broader, more abstract themes that directly relate to your research questions and theoretical framework.

- **Saturation**: Document the point at which new data stops yielding new themes or insights. This is your justification for your qualitative sample size.

- **Trustworthiness and rigor**: Use techniques like **member checking** (sharing findings with participants for validation) and **peer debriefing** (discussing themes with colleagues) to ensure your interpretations are sound.

- **Narrative construction**: Select powerful, representative quotes that illustrate your key themes, forming the textual evidence for your findings.

Interrogating mixed methods data

Mixed methods designs deliberately combine quantitative and qualitative data. The art of this interrogation lies not in running two parallel analyses, but in the specific point of **integration**. Your analysis strategy must rigorously follow the specific design you outlined in your proposal (e.g., Convergent Parallel, Explanatory Sequential).

The core purpose of mixed methods analysis is **triangulation** (checking if results converge) or **complementarity** (exploring different facets of a phenomenon). The integration points—when and how the data streams are connected—determine the power of your findings.

The mixed method analysis process

- **Sequencing (Connecting)**: Use the results from one phase to inform the data collection or analysis of the next. For instance, in an Explanatory Sequential design, you would use statistical outliers or significant quantitative findings to guide the selection of interview participants to better understand *why* the numbers behaved that way.

- **Data transformation (Merging)**: This involves converting one type of data into the other's format for comparison.

- **Quantitizing**: Converting qualitative findings into quantitative data. For example, counting the frequency of emergent themes to see which themes are most prevalent across the sample.

- **Qualitizing**: Converting quantitative findings into qualitative data. For example, using descriptive statistics (like averages or ranges) to select and contextualize quotes or case studies.

- **Joint display (Triangulation)**: Create visual displays (e.g., tables or matrices) where the quantitative results (numbers) and the supporting qualitative themes (quotes) are presented side-by-side. This allows the reader to immediately see convergence, divergence, or complementarity, which is essential for establishing the credibility of mixed findings.

The narrative of interpretation

The analysis phase is complete when you can confidently translate your results (numbers and themes) into defensible findings (what the results mean in context).

- Synthesize, don't just state: Do not simply list p-values or themes. Your job is to connect the results back to the theoretical foundation established in your literature review.

- Address the 'So what?': For every finding, answer the question: What does this contribute to the existing body of knowledge, and how does it change or confirm the theory?

- Limitations first: Acknowledge the limitations of your study (e.g., small sample size, inability to establish causality) *before* celebrating your findings. This establishes scholarly honesty and rigor.

You have successfully moved from a raw collection of data points and transcripts to a set of defensible, insightful findings. These findings are the intellectual currency of your PhD. They are ready to be packaged and presented to the academic world.

The next challenge is translating this analytical work into the formal, argumentative structure of the dissertation itself. **Chapter 25: Writing the core dissertation chapters** will show you how to structure, draft, and polish the Introduction, Literature Review, Methodology, Results, and Discussion chapters to maximize impact and prepare for submission.

25

Writing the core dissertation chapters

Having successfully interrogated your data and generated robust findings, the final structural challenge of Part III is at hand i.e., translating years of effort into a single, cohesive, and highly formal scholarly document- your dissertation draft set up with the core chapters. The dissertation is not a chronological journal of your research journey; it is a meticulously crafted argument that proves your research question is novel, your method is sound, and your findings matter.

This chapter breaks down the five core chapters of the typical dissertation structure, providing strategic guidance on the purpose, tone, and necessary content of each. It also introduces the **continuous writing ethos**, ensuring the dissertation-writing stage is a process of compilation, not creation.

The continuous writing ethos: Starting on day one

The biggest myth surrounding the final phase of the PhD is that writing the dissertation is a separate, monolithic task reserved for the final year. This is a formula for pressure and burnout. The dissertation is an iterative document, and chapters should be started, drafted, and refined throughout the entire doctoral process.

- Treat your literature review as a living document, updating it constantly as you read.
- Draft the Methodology chapter as soon as your proposal is successfully defended. It serves as your execution manual.
- Use the writing process to discover gaps in your logic or data collection, rather than waiting for your committee to point them out.
- Reject the idea of "saving" the writing; the faster you put words down, the faster you move from thinking about research to arguing with evidence.

Now, let's look into the five core chapters of a typical dissertation.

The Introduction chapter: The scholarly pitch

The Introduction is your sales pitch. Its primary goal is to convince the reader (and your committee) within the first few pages that a problem exists, no one else has solved it, or, not to the degree that you will present and you have the (better) solution. It should be written last, after your results and discussion are final, to ensure perfect alignment.

- ***The problem statement***: Start broad, defining the real-world or theoretical problem your field faces. Narrow this down gradually to a specific, researchable gap in the literature. This is where you establish urgency and the need to solve the problem.

- ***The research gap***: State precisely what is missing-mention the gap type you found. Use language like: "While X has been explored, a systematic analysis of Y among Z population remains absent."

- ***The masterful research question***: Explicitly state your main research question, which you developed in Chapter 16.

- ***Statement of contribution***: Briefly summarize the core, unique finding and its significance. (e.g., "This study is the first to establish a causal link between A and B, which has implications for policy X.")

- ***Dissertation framework***: Provide a quick guide to the document structure (e.g., "Chapter 2 provides the literature review, Chapter 3 details the methodology, and so on…"). It is a relatively lengthy document so having a framework helps readers know what to expect when as they read along.

The Literature review chapter: Building your authority

This chapter is your opportunity to demonstrate intellectual mastery over your field. It is a critical, synthesized argument, not a chronological book report. Every paragraph must serve the ultimate goal: justifying the novelty of your research question.

- ***Structure by theme, not Author***: Organize the review around conceptual themes or sub-questions (e.g., "Theories of Burnout in Academia," "Empirical Studies on Scheduling Interventions").

- ***Synthesize and critique***: Do not just summarize what Author A and Author B said. You must critique the work: "While Author A suggests X, this finding relies solely on qualitative data and fails to account for statistical variance, leaving a gap for the current study". You need to weave a story not chronology.

- ***The funnel effect***: Start wide (foundational theories) and narrow down to the specific, most relevant literature that directly leads to the specific gap your study fills.

- ***Theoretical framework***: Explicitly introduce the theoretical framework (e.g., Self-Determination Theory, Sociocultural Theory) that anchors your entire study.

The Methodology chapter: Proving rigor and defensibility

The Methodology chapter is a contract with your reader. It provides the necessary detail for another scholar to replicate your study or, more importantly, for your committee to judge its rigor and ethical compliance. Precision is paramount.

- ***Reaffirm philosophical stance***: Briefly restate your methodological framework (quantitative, qualitative, or mixed-methods) and the philosophy (ontology/episte mology) behind it.

- ***Project-based structure***: If your dissertation follows the **Research Project A and B** schema (see Chapter 18), clearly structure this chapter by project. This is crucial if procedures, sampling, or instruments differ between the two main bodies of work. Given the rigor, you may even have to break this chapter down into parts for the readers.

- ***Participants and setting***: Detail your sampling strategy, inclusion/exclusion criteria, and the size/characteristics of your final sample.

- ***Instruments and measures***: Describe every tool used (surveys, interview protocols, lab equipment), including established psychometric properties (e.g., Cronbach's alpha for reliability).

- ***Procedure***: Provide the step-by-step account of data collection, from recruitment to final data storage (covered in Chapter 23).

- ***Data analysis***: Detail the specific analytical techniques used (e.g., thematic analysis, multiple regression), linking them directly to your stated hypotheses or aims.

The Results chapter: Findings, not interpretations

The Results chapter must be objective, factual, and strictly limited to presenting your empirical findings. Save all interpretation, comparison, and policy implications for the Discussion.

- ***Structure***: Present your findings in a logical order, typically following the sequence of your hypotheses or research aims.

- **Factual presentation:** The results of the planned multi-stage work (**Research Project A** and **Research Project B**), which form the main bulk of your data analysis chapters, should be explicitly presented here, either as separate chapters or clearly distinct sections, to show the successful execution of your multi-stage plan.

- ***Quantitative***: Present descriptive statistics first, followed by the inferential statistics. Use clear, properly labeled tables and figures, and ensure all statistical output is reported in the standardized format of your discipline (e.g., APA, IEEE).

- ***Qualitative***: Present your findings through thematic headings, supported by rich, well-contextualized narrative quotes from your participants.

- ***Zero interpretation***: Do not explain why you think a finding occurred, or how it relates to previous work. Simply state what the data shows (e.g., "A statistically significant difference was observed").

The Discussion chapter: The argument and synthesis

This is your most complex and important chapter, proving your intellectual return on investment. Here, you transition from data presenter to scholar, making a compelling argument for the meaning and impact of your work.

- ***Summary of key findings***: Begin by briefly restating the main results in plain language.

- ***Comparison to literature***: Discuss how your findings agree with, contradict, or extend the existing literature reviewed in Chapter 2. This is where you explain the "why."

- ***Limitations and delimitations***: Honestly and rigorously detail the limitations of your study (e.g., generalizability, sample bias). Delimitations are the choices you made to keep the study focused (e.g., "This study focused solely on US-based data").

- ***Implications and future research***: Detail the theoretical, methodological, and practical implications of your work. Suggest specific directions for future research.

Masterful writing requires managing two narratives: the comprehensive dissertation and the streamlined publication. You have built the comprehensive document. The final phase of your doctoral journey is to move this completed manuscript from a required degree artifact into the successful launch of your career.

You now possess the strategic vision (Part I), the psychological resilience (Part II), and the tactical blueprint (Part III). Part IV begins with **Chapter 26: Mastering the scholarly publication process**, where we strategically address how to compile your dissertation chapters into publishable articles while expertly navigating the delicate boundaries of copyright and self-plagiarism.

IV

The public scholar- Presentation and critique

With the dissertation structure ready, the final challenge is transitioning to a ***public scholar****. This Part focuses on research dissemination and handling critique. We cover* ***Mastering publication****, crafting effective* ***Presentations****, navigating the crucial* ***Feedback loop*** *(positive and negative), managing* ***Setbacks and failures****, understanding* ***Intellectual Property*** *and* ***Data rights****, and successfully traversing the many* ***Ethical minefields*** *of professional research.*

26

Mastering the scholarly publication process

Completing your data analysis is only half the battle. The other half—the one that determines your academic reputation and career trajectory—is dissemination. Getting your findings peer-reviewed and published in respected, indexed journals is the formal mechanism for claiming your contribution to human knowledge.

This chapter shifts your focus from researcher to published author. We'll cover how to navigate the publication landscape across various phases, how to write the key components of a winning manuscript, and how to manage the peer-review cycle.

Phase 1: Strategy and venue selection

Before you even begin writing, you need a strategy. Your dissertation is an archival document; your published articles are the vehicle for sharing your discoveries with the world.

The publication hierarchy

The scholarly impact of a publication on your career is not uniform. Prioritizing output in top-tier venues is critical for your career launch:

- **Tier 1 peer-reviewed Journal (Highest impact):** The gold standard. Demonstrates originality, methodological rigor, and broad field significance. Essential for academic job applications.

- **Tier 2/Specialty peer-reviewed Journal**: Focused, high-quality journals for niche sub-fields. Valuable for specialized impact and volume of output.

- **Peer-reviewed conference proceeding**: Critical for presenting preliminary work, getting early feedback, and building your network. Impact is high for computer science/engineering fields.

- **Book chapter in an edited volume**: Good for synthesizing literature or applying existing data to a new theoretical lens. Impact is lower as chapters are less frequently cited than journal articles.

- **Trade/Industry publication or white paper (Lowest impact)**: Excellent for demonstrating practical impact and engaging non-academic audiences. Minimal scholarly weight on an academic CV.

Selecting the right publication venue

A manuscript is a product, and you must find the right market for it. Selecting the appropriate publication venue such as a conference or an indexed journal is a strategic choice that heavily influences your chances of acceptance.

- **Match scope:** The venue's aims and scope must perfectly align with your research question and field.

- **Assess Impact Factor (IF) / metrics:** Consider the prestige and reach of the venue. Start by targeting publications that are ambitious but realistic for the quality and scope of your current work.

- **Review recent articles:** Read the last two years of published articles. Does your work cite their authors? Do your methods and findings fit the type of research they usually publish?

Spotting and avoiding predatory journals

In the digital age, a malicious publishing model known as **predatory publishing** has emerged. These journals operate solely for profit, charging publication fees without providing legitimate peer review, editorial services, or long-term archiving. Publishing here can severely damage your academic credibility.

Key warning signs to watch for:

- **Fast or non-existent peer review**: They promise acceptance within days or weeks, suggesting no genuine scholarly review is taking place.

- **Aggressive email spam via unofficial channels**: You receive frequent, unsolicited emails inviting you to submit, often containing spelling or grammatical errors.

- **Soliciting manuscripts using unofficial channels** like generic Gmail, Yahoo, or Hotmail addresses is a major red flag. They will constantly bombard and pressurize you if you ever initiate communication.

- **Vague or cloned journal titles**: They adopt names that are either overly broad (e.g., International Journal of Advanced Science) or are cloned names with only a slight adjustment that makes them hard to distinguish from highly respected journals.

- **Poor web design** and functionality: Their websites are often low-quality, poorly maintained, contain numerous typos, and may have broken links or non-functioning submission portals.

- **Fake or misleading Editorial board**: The journal may list high-profile faculty members on its editorial board without their consent. These legitimate scholars have often never mentioned the journal on their professional social profiles (like LinkedIn) or institutional websites.

- **Lack of indexing**: They are not indexed in major, reputable databases relevant to your field (e.g., Web of Science, PubMed, Scopus). Legitimate indexing is a crucial stamp of approval.

- **Pay to publish model**: There will likely be an upfront payment demand as an incentive to get the article published with such venues. No legitimate venue will ask the authors to pay upfront charges and charges are typically not due until the manuscript has been formally approved and typeset for publication.

The Golden rule: If a journal is unknown to you, check it against reputable directories like the Directory of Open Access Journals (DOAJ) or ask senior colleagues for their opinion before submitting.

Essential tools for the publishing scholar

The modern academic relies on specialized software to manage the complex tasks of citing, formatting, and typesetting.

- **Reference management tools**: These tools are non-negotiable. They allow you to collect, organize, and annotate your literature. They handle the instantaneous conversion of your in-text citations and bibliography into any required journal style (e.g., APA, Chicago, Vancouver). These work in tandem with your literature review database that was described in Chapter 15.

- **Document preparation (LaTeX)**: Many fields, especially in STEM, require or strongly prefer that manuscripts be submitted in LaTeX. Overleaf is the premier online collaborative platform for writing in LaTeX, ensuring all equations, figures, and tables are formatted perfectly and can be edited by multiple authors simultaneously. The caveat thus is, access to the internet to save your changes in real time. For instance, your supervisor or you would like to use down time such as when you are on a flight traveling to work on the manuscript but in that case, you would need to make sure the changes are retained till your network connection is restored.

Phase 2: Execution and writing for acceptance

A strong manuscript is about clear, persuasive packaging. The acceptance decision often rests on how well the reviewer can quickly understand the significance of your work.

The Abstract: your elevator pitch

This is the single most important part. It must be a self-contained, structured summary covering: **Context, Aim, Methods, Key results, and Conclusion/Implication.**

The Introduction: Setting the stage

Uses the inverted pyramid structure: moving from the general to the specific, culminating in your research question. It must include a clear statement identifying the **Gap** in the literature that your research is filling.

The Methodology: The reproducibility mandate

Must contain enough granular detail for another competent researcher to **replicate** your study exactly. Justify all major choices (e.g., sample selection, statistical tests).

Results and discussion: The narrative of discovery

The **Results** section must be purely objective, presenting findings with precision (e.g., p-values, effect sizes).

The **Discussion** is where you transition back to a scholar, interpreting your findings, comparing them to the literature, and detailing the **Implications** and **Limitations** of your work.

Figures and Tables: The visual argument

Visual elements are often the first thing reviewers look at, and they must be **stand-alone**, capable of telling the story of your findings without reference to the text.

Do:

- Stand-alone clarity: Ensure the caption and the visual element (figure or table) contain enough information for a reader to understand the result without reading the body text.
- Simplicity: Remove all non-essential ink and lines. A complex idea presented simply is professional; a simple idea presented complexly is confusing.
- Consistency: Use consistent formatting, fonts, and color palettes across all visuals.
- Compliance: Always ensure your figures and tables are in compliance with guidelines set forth by the publication venue.

Don't:

- Duplicate data: Do not present the same numbers in both a table and a figure. Choose the best visual format (table for precision, figure for trends/relationships).
- Use default software output: Never paste raw output from statistical software; always custom-format visuals to journal specifications.
- Hide error: For quantitative data, always include error bars or confidence intervals to honestly represent the uncertainty of your estimate.

You have written an impactful manuscript, you have been warned of the predatory publications so how do you decide which tier of publication your manuscript should be submitted to and what's the process like? These are some aspects that we will look into next.

Phase 3: The formal review cycle

The publication cycle is slow and emotionally demanding. Knowing the stages helps manage expectations.

The publication process: A strategic timeline

Here are the typical steps from submission to publication:

Submission: The work is formally sent to the journal editor.

They conduct an initial desk review to check for fit.

Peer Review (Under Review): If your manuscript contributions and theme fit the overall scope and aim of the publication venue, the paper is sent to 2–3 expert reviewers. This stage typically takes 3 to 12 months, depending on the field and type of submission- shorter for conferences and longer for journals. This long waiting time is a key factor in the rising popularity of pre-prints.

The Decision (Major/Minor/Reject):

Once the manuscript has been thoroughly reviewed you will be given a decision in one of the following forms:

Major Revision and Re-submission (R&R): The most common outcome for good work. The paper is promising but requires substantial changes, re-analysis, or new experiments. This is a positive sign, requiring a strong response letter.

Minor Revision: Requires small, quick fixes (e.g., grammatical changes, minor clarifications). Acceptance is highly likely after these are addressed.

Rejection: Common, even for strong papers. Always use the reviewer feedback to immediately revise and submit to the next journal on your list.

Acceptance: The paper is formally accepted, followed by proofing and formatting.

Publication: The paper is officially posted online (often with an "in press" designation).

The confidentiality of peer review: Single-blind vs. Double-blind

The peer review stage is critical to scientific validation, and it operates under strict rules of confidentiality to minimize bias. The "blindness" refers to who knows whose identity: the authors', the reviewers', or both.

Single-blind review

Mechanism: The reviewers know the author's identity (name, institution, prior work), but the author does not know the reviewers' identities.

Pros: This method allows reviewers to evaluate the current manuscript in the context of the author's established expertise or prior work, which can sometimes lead to a more accountable review.

Cons: It carries a higher risk of bias—either conscious or unconscious—based on the author's reputation, institutional prestige, or even gender/ethnic background.

Double-blind review

Mechanism: Neither the reviewers nor the authors know each other's identities. The manuscript is submitted without author names, affiliations, or identifying self-references (e.g., "In our prior work [1]...").

Pros: This method maximizes objectivity, ensuring the manuscript is judged strictly on its scientific merit, methods, and contribution, regardless of who wrote it. This is the standard in many social sciences and humanities fields.

Cons: It can be difficult to maintain perfectly, as reviewers in highly specialized fields may still be able to deduce authorship from the research topic or citation patterns.

The Rebuttal: Mastering the response letter

When you receive a decision of **Major** or **Minor Revision** (R&R), you must submit a revised manuscript and an accompanying **rebuttal** (or response letter). This document is often as critical to acceptance as the revised paper itself, as it demonstrates your professionalism and your ability to engage constructively with criticism.

The rebuttal is a formal, line-by-line response to *every single comment* made by every reviewer and the editor. Here is how to approach a rebuttal letter:

- Maintain a **professional tone**: Always begin by thanking the reviewers for their time and valuable feedback. Keep the tone respectful, positive, and collaborative, even when disagreeing with a point.

- **Structure** and detail: Create a separate section for each reviewer's comments. Copy the reviewer's original comment verbatim (often in italics or quotes), and then provide your response directly beneath it.

- **Cross-reference** changes: For every change made, state exactly what you did and provide the page number and line numbers in the revised manuscript where the change can be found (e.g., "We added a sentence clarifying the limitation on page 14, lines 345-350"). You can even color code the changes to make them stand out from the unedited text.

- **Justify** defenses: If you choose not to make a requested change (which is sometimes necessary), politely and scientifically justify your reasoning. You must convince the editor that your original choice was the correct one for the paper's integrity.

Understanding the causes of rejections

You have poured your heart and soul into the manuscript. You prepared it for acceptance, yet, you got the hard news—Rejection. Given the single and double-blind confidentiality, your manuscript needs to speak for itself and make an impact. If it fails to do that, here are some of the common reasons why:

- Weak/**misaligned novelty** claims: The introduction section of the manuscript is where you as an author have an opportunity to make an impact by claiming your novelty. You need to explicitly spell out contributions and the significance thereof. If you fail to explicitly communicate or claim to have done more than what you actually did, the journal will likely reject your manuscript.

- **Misaligned scope** of contributions: Early on in your Introduction, you highlight the problem and its urgency. If you fail to limit the scope of the problem early in the narrative, but later, your Methodology only addresses a partial scope of the problem, the manuscript will be rejected for falling short of its own defined goals. This is a crucial mismatch between problem framing and solution delivery.

- **Weak empirical evidence**: Making claims about your contributions is one thing but proving the worth of your contributions is another. You need to thoroughly present and discuss the empirical findings to prove that your methodology competes and outperforms the state of the art when evaluated on standardized metrics. Failing to provide sufficient empirical evidence is another cause of rejection.

- **Chaotic manuscript** organization: Ever stumbled upon

a manuscript where the story line and contributions felt like it was all over the place? You likely won't find this with a tier 1 or 2 publication as it will be rejected. This is more about your ability to structure the manuscript such that it follows a logical flow. For instance, problem statement → urgency → state of the art (SOTA) contributions → limitations of SOTA → your novel contributions → methodology → empirical findings and discussions → conclusion and future works. If you jumble this chronology, your manuscript will be rejected. Caveat: At times, your manuscript will have to break this chronology to adhere to the publication guidelines but even then, the organization and clarity are critical for highlighting your work.

- **Poor presentation** and low impact abstract: Your paper shouldn't only be theoretically and fundamentally sound, but it should be written to make an impact. The editor's first impression is based on your Abstract and Title. You must give them a bold reason to continue reading—the problem is worth solving, there is urgency, and you solved it. If your manuscript fails to make a strong first impression itself, the odds will be stacked up against you.

Understanding the reasons for rejection helps inform your re-submission strategy and highlights the need to protect your work before it is even submitted. When and if you receive a rejection, it will sting but don't take it to heart and remember the tool: The 24-Hour rule for resilience that was previously mentioned in Chapter 8 to help you get past this feeling.

Phase 4: Acceleration and Integration

As you move toward your final dissertation, you must protect your work while making it visible.

Pre-prints: Accelerating dissemination

Pre-prints (e.g., arXiv) allow you to establish priority and get rapid feedback before formal peer review. However, they are not a quality guarantee and carry the risk of public scrutiny before the work is fully vetted.

When and how to use them

- **Establish priority**: The main reason to use a pre-print is to immediately establish the date of your discovery, protecting your intellectual claim in fast-moving fields (e.g., Physics, Computer Science, Biology).

- **Rapid feedback**: They allow you to get rapid, public feedback from the global community, which you can use to improve the manuscript before formal journal submission.

- **Journal policy check**: Always check the specific journal's policy before posting a pre-print. While most top-tier journals are "pre-print friendly," some specialized journals may still consider pre-printing to violate their originality rules.

Pros and Cons of pre-print submissions

The decision to post a pre-print involves weighing the benefits of speed against the risks of exposure.

Pros (Why to use them):

- **Speed and priority**: Provides instant dissemination and establishes an immediate public timestamp for your research.

- **Open access**: Guarantees your work is openly accessible to all researchers, bypassing journal paywalls.

- **Early citation**: Allows you and others to cite the work months or years before formal journal publication.

Cons (Potential drawbacks):

- **No quality guarantee**: The work lacks the definitive certification of rigor provided by formal peer review, meaning the reader must be cautious.

- **Misinterpretation risk**: Preliminary findings carry a higher risk of being misinterpreted by the press, public, or policy-makers, especially in sensitive or controversial research areas.

- **Public scrutiny**: If the work contains flaws, they will be exposed publicly, and the record cannot easily be erased (pre-prints can be retracted, but the history usually remains).

The Dissertation embargo

Since your dissertation becomes a public record, immediate release can sometimes be considered "prior publication" by high-impact journals. A strategic embargo (1–5 years) seals your dissertation while your manuscripts are still in the review cycle.

Integrating publications: The "Sandwich" dissertation

When compiling published articles into a dissertation, you must bridge the chapters to create a single voice. Expand the truncated literature reviews of the articles and ensure notations are consistent throughout the entire document.

Avoiding self-plagiarism

You must treat your own published work as if it were written by another scholar. Obtain written permission from the publisher to reuse the material and always paraphrase and re-write the text rather than copying and pasting from your own papers.

Understanding the formal review process, embargo and the accelerated routes like pre-prints is essential for effectively launching your research into the global scholarly conversation. By mastering dissemination, you transition from someone who does research to someone who shares and influences as a published author. Successfully navigating copyright, avoiding self-plagiarism, and understanding how to package your findings are the key components of a successful publication strategy.

You have now established the philosophical, practical, and editorial foundation for your work. Your final step in preparation is learning how to present these findings—whether in a manuscript or on a stage—and how to handle the inevitable critique. **Chapter 27, Receiving and responding to critique**, will walk you through managing and responding to critique both for manuscript submitted for publications and for your dissertation.

27

Receiving and responding to critique

Preparing a manuscript is one thing but the acceptance of the manuscript as a scholarly publication is rarely a straight line. It involves navigating critique-sometimes harsh too.

Feedback is not a judgment on your intelligence or worth, but a vital mechanism for improving your research and sharpening your arguments. Mastering the art of receiving and responding to formal critique transforms a good piece of research into a great one.

Navigating feedback for publications (Peer review)

Peer review is the crucible of scholarly publishing. It is often a harsh but necessary process designed to test your paper's robustness and theoretical contribution.

The mindset: Detaching self from work

When you receive a decision (whether rejection, major revisions, or minor revisions), the first rule is to **separate the criticism from your identity.** Reviewers critique the *work,* not the *author.*

- ***Read once, walk away***: Your initial reading of reviewer comments will likely trigger an emotional response (anger, defensiveness, or confusion). Read the comments once quickly to understand the general verdict, and then put them away for at least 24 hours (***Tool: The 24-Hour rule for resilience***). Do not respond or plan your revision until you are operating from a calm, analytical perspective.

- ***The "Reviewer 2" phenomenon*:** Every author has encountered the infamous **"Reviewer 2,"** whose comments seem overly harsh, dismissive, or demand entirely new research. Accept that this is a near-universal experience. When faced with this kind of critique, double down on the first rule: **step away.** The critique might sting, but it often contains the kernel of the most significant—if painful—improvement needed.

- ***Acknowledge the intent***: Assume the reviewer's intent is to improve your paper. Even when the tone is brusque, look for the underlying, constructive point they are trying to make.

The strategy: Structured response and revision

Your response document is just as important as your revision. It proves to the editor and reviewers that you have taken every comment seriously and acted on it professionally.

Categorize the critique: Go through the comments and categorize them by impact:

- **Major/Conceptual**: Requires new analysis, data collection, or a complete restructuring of the argument. (These often determine acceptance.)
- **Minor/Editorial**: Requires copy edits, citation checks, word choice changes, or simple clarification of existing text.
- **Contradictory**: When two reviewers ask for opposing changes (e.g., "shorten the literature review" vs. "expand the literature review").

The point-by-point response: Create a separate document that addresses every single comment individually. This response should be comprehensive, polite, and direct.

- **Quote the comment**: Copy the original reviewer comment.

- **State your action**: Summarize what you did (e.g., "We agreed with this suggestion and have added a new paragraph to page 12, lines 301-305, addressing X.")

- **Explain your rationale** (If needed): If you disagree with a comment, politely but firmly explain why your original approach serves the paper's core objective better, referencing established literature to support your defense. Never simply ignore a comment.

Handling rejection (Revise and Resubmit elsewhere): If your paper is outright rejected, immediately focus on the most insightful reviewer comments. Use them to improve the manuscript and target a slightly different, equally prestigious venue for re-submission. Do not discard the work—it is now a stronger paper because of the review process and has received preliminary validation too.

Successfully navigating the peer review process—whether through major revisions or a re-submission after rejection—is the most challenging part of academic publishing. You've endured the fire of critique and forged a stronger, clearer piece of research. This journey confirms your work is robust and ready for the world. You can now shift your focus from rebuttal to delivery.

The next step isn't just seeing your paper in print; it's maximizing the impact of that achievement. We'll look at how to leverage your new publication to advance your career and disseminate your findings effectively. The hard part of the scholarship is done; now comes the part about building your reputation and presenting in front of an audience.

28

Presenting your accepted work with purpose

Congratulations—you have responded well to critique and finally your manuscript is accepted! The next step is often presenting that work at a major conference. Unlike the dissertation defense (aimed at proving competence to an internal committee), the **conference presentation** is a crucial, high-stakes opportunity aimed at influencing your peers, establishing your profile, and opening doors for career advancement. This chapter focuses on how to leverage the 10-20 minutes you have on stage to make a lasting professional impact.

Creating the research impact package

Few people outside your field will read a dense, 8,000-word article. To maximize reach, you need to create user-friendly assets that translate your findings for various audiences. This is your **Impact Package**.

- **Develop a Plain Language Summary (PLS):** Write a 200-word summary that uses clear, accessible language, free of jargon. Structure it as **Problem, Method, Key Finding, and conclusion/impact**. This PLS is what you will use for social media, email announcements, and press releases.

- **Design a key visual/figure:** Identify the single most important graph, table, or schematic from your paper. If possible, create a slightly cleaned-up, high-resolution version specifically for sharing on social platforms. Visuals drive engagement much more effectively than text alone.

- **Draft the "Elevator Pitch":** Create three versions of your paper's summary: a single, punchy sentence; a 60-second verbal summary; and a three-point bulleted list of the main takeaways. This prepares you for both casual conversations and professional networking.

Strategic dissemination pre-presentation

Don't just wait for the paper to appear; actively push it out to the communities that need to see it to create some hype especially among attendees who will likely be at the conference venue where this work is to be presented.

- **The social media blast:** Use your PLS and Key Visual (or the official journal link) to announce the paper on relevant platforms (e.g., X/Twitter, LinkedIn). Tag your co-authors, the journal, your institution, and any relevant professional organizations or funders. Use strategic hashtags to ensure discoverability.

- **Email signature update:** Add a line to your professional email signature: "New Publication: [Paper Title] (In Press/Published in [Journal Name]) [Link/DOI]."

- **Direct email announcement:** Send a personalized, concise email to colleagues, collaborators, professors, and professionals who work in your niche. Briefly state the main finding and provide the link. Do not send a mass email; curate a focused list.

- **Presentations and conferences:** Leverage the accepted work by proposing talks or posters at upcoming conferences aside from the main talk about your work. Presenting the research in person is one of the most effective ways to generate buzz, get early citations, and meet future collaborators.

The purpose of the presentation: Piquing interest

Forget trying to summarize your entire 8,000-word paper in a 15-minute slot. That approach leaves the audience overwhelmed, confused, and bored.

The true goal of a conference presentation is to **pique interest** and provide a clear, compelling **"Why."** Your time on stage is not the final word; it is the **advertisement** for your paper. The real success of a presentation is measured by the quality of the intellectual conversations and networking opportunities you generate *after* the session ends.

To achieve this, focus on **storytelling** over data enumeration. Instead of being *thorough* (covering every analysis and limitation), be **focused**, highlighting only the most significant finding and its major implication. Your presentation should aim at **starting the conversation**, not ending it, by leaving the audience with a provocative question or a call for collaboration.

Presenting with authority

Your delivery should be professional, confident, and engaging.

Skip memorizing the speech

It is tempting to write out your entire speech and commit it to memory. However, highly rehearsed or memorized speeches fall apart easily when faced with minor distractions, nerves, or an unexpected audience question.

- ***The cue card trap***: While cue cards are tempting for initial structure, they are a liability for a nervous speaker. If you drop them in the middle of a speech, the interruption to gather them will be far more distracting than simply speaking from your slides.

- ***Use slides as your anchor***: Your presentation slides should serve as your teleprompter and visual aid. Each slide title should be your main talking point. Use **minimal text** and focus on powerful, **clear visuals** (figures, diagrams) to guide you through the narrative. **Never read directly from the slides**.

- ***Practice talking points, not text***: Practice speaking to the slides using bullet points or key phrases, focusing on the flow between ideas, not the exact wording. This allows you to maintain eye contact and speak naturally.

Dos and Don'ts: Your high-impact presentation checklist

Following these actionable points will elevate your presentation from a summary to a performance.

The Do's of an engaging presentation

- ***Focus on the core narrative***: Every slide should answer the question: "Why does this matter?" Use the presentation to tell the story of your research journey, from the puzzle you faced to the solution you found.

- ***Visualize data***: Replace lengthy tables and dense paragraphs with clean, high-contrast figures and charts. The audience should be able to grasp the main finding of a visual element in under 10 seconds.

- ***Pre-empt the Q&A***: Dedicate a few backup slides at the end of your deck (hidden during the main presentation) to address likely questions. For example, have a slide ready with extra detail on your methodology, boundary conditions, or sensitivity analysis. This allows you to pull up data instantly when a specific, predictable question arises, showcasing confidence and preparation.

- ***Maintain eye contact***: Scan the audience to create connection. Pick three points in the room (left, center, right) and rotate your gaze naturally.

- ***Repeat the question***: Always repeat or rephrase the question for the audience and, critically, for yourself. This gives you a moment to process the question and ensures everyone knows what you're addressing.

The Don'ts of a detrimental presentation

- ***No walls of text***: Never put a large block of text on a slide. If you need to include a quote or a key phrase, limit it to one concise, impactful sentence. Remember, if the audience is reading, they are not listening to you.

- ***Never read from the slides***: Your slides are visual aids, not scripts. Reading the text that is simultaneously displayed is redundant and signals a lack of preparation or confidence. Talk to your slides, not at them.

- ***Avoid over-jargon***: While presenting to experts, ensure you define acronyms and complex terms, especially in the first few minutes, to welcome attendees from adjacent fields.

- ***Handle unknowns gracefully***: If you receive a question where you genuinely don't know the answer, avoid guessing or apologizing excessively. Instead, pivot the question back to the research direction: "That's a fascinating tangent—it's outside the scope of this particular study, but it gives us a clear direction for Future Work, perhaps focusing on [State the concept/variable they mentioned]." This frames your gap in knowledge as a planned research trajectory.

Technical preparedness: The triple backup rule

Technical glitches are the single most common threat to a successful presentation. You must prepare for any and all sorts of technical difficulties.

The Triple Backup Rule: Always have **multiple backups** of your **final slides**:

- **Primary**: On a USB drive, formatted as both a PDF and a PowerPoint/Keynote file.

- **Secondary**: Saved to a cloud service (e.g., Google Drive,

Dropbox) that you can access on any device via a web browser.

- **Tertiary**: Emailed to yourself or a trusted co-author who is also at the conference.

Adapter check: The conference venue's technology is often unpredictable. Always bring your own necessary adapters (especially USB-C/Thunderbolt to HDMI/VGA). Never assume the provided equipment will match your laptop.

Anticipate display issues: Design your slides for a 16:9 aspect ratio, but prepare a backup version in the older 4:3 format just in case the projector defaults to it.

Embed fonts: If you use unusual fonts, embed them in your presentation file to ensure they render correctly on a different computer. If that's impossible, use universally supported fonts like Arial, Helvetica, or Times New Roman.

Networking for everyone: A guide for introverts

A conference is not just about the paper session; it's about the **networking opportunities** that can lead to collaborations, job interviews, and future funding. For introverts, the thought of "working a room" can be exhausting, but success requires strategic effort.

Strategic networking tips

1. **Quality over quantity**: Focus on having 2-3 deep, meaningful conversations rather than dozens of superficial exchanges.

2. **Use research as the icebreaker**: You have an accepted paper—leverage it! Approach someone whose work you admire and say, "I saw your presentation/paper on [Specific Topic]. I was particularly interested in your method for [Specific Detail]. My research on [Your Topic] has a similar challenge..."

3. **Utilize poster sessions**: Poster sessions are excellent for introverts. They naturally facilitate one-on-one or small-group discussions, reducing the pressure of large crowds. Stand by your poster and engage with those who approach you.

4. **Scheduled meetings**: Use email or LinkedIn before the conference to schedule brief, informal coffee meetings with specific faculty members or researchers you want to meet. This avoids the chaotic hunt and provides a structured conversation environment.

5. **Use food as a shield**: Attend networking receptions and meals. Having a drink or a plate of food in your hands gives you a visual focal point and a non-awkward reason to stand alone, allowing you to observe and choose your interactions deliberately.

Your work has been accepted, presented, and critically engaged with. Your presence at the conference, combined with a confident presentation, solidifies your position as a credible expert in your field. Remember: This is your time to make an indelible mark in the minds of the people who matter most to your future. For this, you need to establish a digital scholarly profile to make it easier for people to find you, your work and to keep in touch. Your work and contributions should live on past that conference. You can achieve this by establishing a digital scholar profile which is what we will address next.

29

Building your digital scholarly identity

After you've successfully presented your accepted work—be at it at any venue that will publicly index your contributions—the next critical task is ensuring that your contribution lives on and remains easily discoverable. Your research can't have impact if it can't be found.

In the modern academic and professional landscape, your physical presence is fleeting, but your **digital scholarly identity** is permanent. Building this presence is one of the most strategic things you can do to future-proof your career. This chapter describes two prominent ways to build and maintain your digital scholarly identity.

Mastering your Google scholar profile

Beyond simply listing your papers, this profile provides crucial visual and numerical data:

- **Key metrics:** The profile prominently displays your **total citation count**, which is a cumulative count of every time any of your indexed papers has been cited. It also shows the **H-index** (which measures both productivity and citation impact—e.g., an H-index of 10 means 10 papers cited at least 10 times) and the **i10-index** (the count of papers with at least 10 citations).

- **Citation growth visualization:** A **graph showing citation growth over the years** is automatically generated. This visual representation allows others to quickly gauge the long-term trajectory and continued relevance of your work.

- **Co-authors:** The **list of co-authors** links your profile to your professional network. This section is vital for displaying your collaborative history and showing the breadth of your interdisciplinary connections.

Papers are added to your profile primarily through **automatic indexation** when the Google Scholar crawler finds your work on a reliable academic server (like a journal website or institutional repository). However, you must actively **manually check and add** any missing or mis-attributed publications to ensure accuracy. It is normal for it to take some time—sometimes several weeks or months—for your newest publications to appear in the index, and that's perfectly okay.

Caveat. While metrics like the H-index and i10-index offer quick snapshots of your productivity, treat them as **vanity metrics**. Do not get fixated on constantly improving them or, worse, manipulating them with self citations. The true purpose of the profile is professional verification and discoverability; obsessing over a slightly higher number distracts from the core work of research. Focus on the quality of your publications and the maintenance of an accurate, comprehensive list.

Personal website over business cards for networking

While a physical business card has its place in networking, it is a static artifact that provides minimal information and needs to be physically exchanged.

A **personal academic website** is a dynamic, twenty-four-seven networking tool that far surpasses the utility of a card. It acts as the central hub for your entire scholarly identity, serving as the definitive answer to the question: "Who is this researcher, and what have they accomplished?"

Your website doesn't need to be complex or expensive; even a free, single-page site is sufficient to start. The crucial functions of this site are to host:

1. Your current **Curriculum Vitae (CV)** or résumé.
2. A clear, professional **headshot**.

3. A list of your **publications** with links to the full text or official record.
4. A statement of your **research interests** and a summary of your PhD project.
5. Easy-to-find **contact information** (beware of incoming **SPAM**!!).

Unlike a CV or résumé, a website allows you to control the narrative of your work and provides essential context for potential collaborators, employers, and future students. It is the platform from which you actively shape your personal brand, making you a more visible and accessible public scholar.

Sharing findings beyond peer-reviewed publications

The traditional model of research—keeping findings private until peer-reviewed publication—is rapidly giving way to **Open Scholarship**. Platforms like blogging and professional social media allow you to engage with your community, establish expertise, and make your research discoverable *before* it hits the journals.

Blogging vs. scientific publication

Scientific publication and academic blogging serve fundamentally different purposes, yet they are both critical components of a modern scholarly brand. You should view them not as competing tasks, but as two parts of a unified communication strategy.

The primary goal of a **Scientific Publication** is **formal validation** and contributing to the official academic record. These are slow, archived, and retrospective documents; they present final, methodology-driven results that have been rigorously scrutinized by subject-matter experts during peer review. The tone is objective, highly formal, and standardized. This process is how you establish **authority** and **rigour**, providing the official *proof* of your contribution.

In stark contrast, a **blog post** or professional social media activity is fast, immediate, and its main goal is **conversation** and building a visible public audience. Its style is conversational and accessible, often including opinion or pedagogical elements aimed at a broader audience, including students, journalists, and interdisciplinary scholars. This is how you establish your **voice** and **accessibility**, controlling the narrative and demonstrating the immediate relevance of your work to the wider world.

Benefits of actively sharing your findings

Active sharing of your research journey and preliminary findings (always adhering to institutional guidelines) offers powerful benefits. Firstly, it provides a clear, time-stamped public record of your intellectual progress, establishing your **priority** in the research area. Secondly, when you share your work, you generate immediate traction, allowing for mentions and shares, and signaling early interest. Finally, sharing preliminary data allows experts outside your immediate circle to offer quick, informal feedback, which can catch errors, suggest new analytical approaches, and ultimately strengthen your final published paper.

Overcoming the fear of theft

The most common concern scholars have is the fear of being "scooped"—that if they share a novel idea, a competitor will steal it and publish first. This fear often stems from an overestimation of the idea's value and an underestimation of the work required for execution.

The truth is, almost no research idea is 100% unique. Given the fast paced research in most disciplines and the sheer volume of researchers around the globe working on pushing research frontiers, there are always more than one person thinking about the same idea.

The true intellectual property of your doctoral work lies not in the initial concept, but in the **flawless execution** of the methodology, the painstaking data collection, the nuanced analysis, and the synthesis of the results. This represents hundreds of hours of work that cannot be replicated quickly. Ironically, *not sharing* your work leaves your ideas vulnerable. By posting about your methods, data collection progress, and preliminary findings, you create an undeniable public record, and the rigor of your **execution** is your strongest defense against imitators.

This commitment to publicly broadcasting your work and brand is essential. However, once you start leveraging these public channels—actively blogging and sharing preliminary findings—you must understand the rules governing the content and be prepared to defend the intellectual property contained within them. Our next step is to safeguard the **intellectual rights** of your contributions along with copyright, and data management.

30

Intellectual property, Copyright, and data rights

The acceptance of your research paper transforms your manuscript from a private academic document into a public, copyrighted asset. Before you proceed to integrate that work into your final dissertation structure (a process often called a "sandwich dissertation"), you must address the administrative and legal requirements of Intellectual Property (IP), copyright, and data management.

This is a mandatory step. Failing to secure the correct reuse permissions can result in your university rejecting your dissertation submission or, worse, running into legal issues with the **publisher (whether a journal or a conference proceeding)**.

Navigating publication copyright and reuse permissions (Journals and Conferences)

When your paper was accepted, you almost certainly signed a **Copyright Transfer Agreement (CTA)** or a Publishing Agreement. This document determines your rights and obligations, whether the publication is in a journal or a conference proceeding.

Understanding manuscript versions and dissertation reuse

Before integrating your work, you must determine which version of the paper you are legally allowed to include in your dissertation. Each stage of the manuscript carries a different copyright risk:

- **Preprint Version:** This is the original manuscript you submitted before any peer review took place. It is generally the **safest and lowest-risk version** to use in your dissertation, as the publisher has no copyright claim on this unreviewed content.

- **Author Accepted Manuscript (AAM) / Camera-ready/ Post-Print:** This version is the result of the manuscript after peer review changes and all corrections have been implemented, but before the publisher has applied their professional formatting and typesetting. This is typically the **best and most common option** for dissertation inclusion. Most major publishers grant automatic reuse rights for the AAM, but you **must**

confirm with the specific publisher's policy.

- **Version of Record (VoR) / Publisher's PDF:** This is the final, professionally typeset, formatted, and published PDF that appears in the journal or conference proceedings. Using this version, or specific figures taken from it, is **High Risk** and requires you to secure **explicit, written permission** from the publisher's Permissions Department, as this version is fully owned by the publisher.

The dissertation clause and publisher policies

Most publishers (journal and conference alike) understand that papers are often the basis for a PhD dissertation. This is usually covered by one of two mechanisms:

1. **The Institutional/Dissertation Clause:** Many CTAs have a built-in clause stating that the author retains the right to use the work in a non-commercial dissertation or dissertation. **Check your signed agreement first.** If this clause exists, you usually only need to cite the paper formally.

2. **Publisher Policy Aggregators:** If the clause is absent or unclear, use the **publisher policy aggregator** database. Search for the journal or conference name; the resulting entry will explicitly state the publisher's policy on reusing the AAM or VoR in a dissertation.

Securing formal written permission

If your policy check indicates the reuse right is not automatically granted or if you want to use the **Version of Record (VoR)**, you must get permission:

- **Who to contact:** Email the publisher's **Permissions Department** (not the editor).
- **What to request:** State clearly that you are the author/co-author and require non-exclusive, non-commercial permission to reproduce the accepted manuscript (or specific figures/text) as a chapter in your doctoral dissertation, which will be submitted to the university repository. The same applies in case of use for commercial permission in which case suitable license fees will apply.
- **Documentation: Retain the email approval/license grant permanently.** You must be prepared to present this documentation to your university's Graduate School upon submission.

Managing Intellectual Property (IP) and Invention Disclosure

For research that involves novel methods, software, or potential commercial value, this is the time to formalize your IP status.

- **Invention Disclosure:** If your project produced a novel or patentable idea (a new algorithm, material, diagnostic tool, etc.) that was *not* fully disclosed in the publication, contact your university's **Technology Transfer Office (TTO)** immediately.

- **Why now?** Disclosing the invention *after* publication can sometimes complicate patent applications in certain jurisdictions, as the work is already public. The TTO can help you determine if a provisional patent needs to be filed immediately to secure the intellectual property before the paper is widely disseminated.

- **Software and Code:** If the published work relies on custom software or code, decide whether you plan to open-source it (using licenses like MIT or GPL) or if the IP should be protected by the university. Consult your TTO.

Data archival and integrity

Your responsibility to your published work extends to ensuring the integrity and reproducibility of the underlying data.

- **Data archival requirements:** Review the publisher's data availability policy. You may be required to deposit your raw, processed, or analysis code in a public, persistent repository (e.g., Zenodo, Figshare, Dryad).

- **Metadata and README:** Ensure that the deposited data is accompanied by clear **metadata** and a detailed **README file** explaining how to access and use the data, linking it directly to the published paper's DOI.

- **Data Management Plan (DMP) check:** Revisit the Data Management Plan you created at the start of your research (Chapter 23). Verify that all original data are stored securely and backed up according to institutional policy.

Securing permissions and formalizing your IP status are administrative safety nets that safeguard your academic career and your dissertation submission. This preparation clears the path of all potential legal and administrative obstacles. Before moving into the writing phase, the next crucial step is understanding and navigating ethical minefields.

31

Navigating ethical minefields

The pursuit of a PhD requires not only intellectual rigor but also uncompromising ethical integrity. Academic ethics are the invisible lines that protect the validity of your research and the credibility of your career. Ethical compliance extends far beyond securing initial approval from the Institutional Review Board (IRB) or Ethics Committee. As you finalize your research and begin integrating published results into your final dissertation, you enter a phase where issues of authorship, data integrity, privacy, and conflict of interest become critical. An ethical lapse can lead to the retraction of your work, the forfeiture of your degree, and a permanent stain on your professional reputation.

This chapter defines the major ethical pitfalls in modern doctoral work and provides a strategy for proactive defense, ensuring your work is beyond reproach.

Reaffirming ethical approval and protocol compliance

Your final dissertation is a public record of your entire research journey. You must confirm that all human or animal data used (if any) adheres strictly to the originally approved protocol.

Scope check: Did your project drift?

Review your original ethics approval letter. Did your methodology or data collection shift significantly during the research process?

If you made minor changes (e.g., sample size adjustment), ensure these changes were reported to the IRB as required by your institution.

If you made major changes (e.g., added a new intervention or a new population) you must confirm that you received a formal protocol amendment approval. No data obtained under a non-approved protocol can be included.

Consent integrity

Confirm that you can demonstrate proper consent procedures were followed for all included participants. This is especially important if you are referencing participant quotes or case studies.

Withdrawal: If a participant withdrew consent, ensure their data was properly removed from all analyses and final datasets.

Anonymization: Double-check that all identifying personal information (PII) has been removed from the final data used in the dissertation.

The authorship minefield: Defining roles and responsibilities

When including a published paper with co-authors in your dissertation, authorship attribution must be handled with transparency and fairness.

The criteria for authorship

To be listed as an author, you must have contributed to **all four** of the following points:

1. **Substantial contributions** to the conception or design of the work; or the acquisition, analysis, or interpretation of data for the work;
2. **Drafting the work or revising** it critically for important intellectual content;
3. **Final approval** of the version to be published; and
4. Agreement to be **accountable** for all aspects of the work.

Handling disputes proactively

- Acknowledge non-authors: Individuals who provided only technical help, writing assistance, or administrative support (e.g., funding acquisition, general supervision) should be listed in the Acknowledgements section, not as authors.

- Required confirmation: Before submission, it is best practice to send the final manuscript draft (or the chapter integrating the paper) to all co-authors for their final approval. This prevents last-minute disagreements about content or attribution.

Navigating self-citation and the metrics minefield

Self-citation is the act of referencing a paper or work that you previously authored. This is frequently a legitimate and necessary practice, but it is also one of the most tempting areas for ethical abuse if done merely to inflate personal metrics.

When self-citation is required

Citing your own previous work is appropriate and essential when:

1. **Establishing context:** Your current paper builds directly on a specific methodology, model, or finding you introduced earlier.
2. **Methodological necessity:** You are using a tool, dataset, or technique that you were the first to develop or validate in a prior publication.

The self-citation should always be the **most relevant and**

necessary source for the point you are making.

Avoiding metric manipulation

The ethical line is crossed when you use **excessive or unnecessary self-citations** simply to artificially boost your **total citation count** or **H-index**.

- **The ethical mandate:** Do not include a self-citation if a neutral source would serve the purpose equally well, or if the citation is not critical for the reader's understanding of your current argument.

- **The cost of gaming:** Attempts to artificially inflate metrics are often seen as a form of **citation manipulation** or **metric gaming**. Research institutions and journals are increasingly vigilant about this behavior, and discovery can severely damage your academic integrity. Focus on the *quality* and *relevance* of your citations, not the *quantity* of your score.

The core ethical violations: Plagiarism and research fraud

Research misconduct is the most serious ethical breach and can result in severe academic and professional penalties. Your dissertation is the ultimate testament to your integrity as a scholar, and it must be free of these offenses.

Offense 1: Plagiarism (Theft of ideas or words- including your own)

Plagiarism is the appropriation of another person's ideas, processes, results, or words without giving appropriate credit.

- **Standard plagiarism**: Copying text, graphics, or unique ideas from any external source (published papers, websites, books) without proper citation or quotation marks.

- **Self-plagiarism (Redundancy)**: Reusing substantial portions of your own previously published work (the papers forming your dissertation chapters) without proper internal citation and an explanatory statement. This is a common trap in "sandwich theses" and must be strictly managed.

Offense 2: Data falsification and fabrication

These two acts collectively constitute the manipulation of the research record.

- **Falsification**: Manipulating research materials, equipment, or processes, or changing or omitting data or results such that the research is not accurately represented in the research record. (E.g., deleting outliers that contradict your hypothesis, selectively reporting findings).

- **Fabrication**: Making up data or results and recording or reporting them. (E.g., inventing survey responses, generating data points where none existed).

Guidelines for integrating published work (Avoiding self-plagiarism)

When integrating a published chapter:

- **Always use introductory text**: Start the chapter with a clear, mandatory statement explaining that the following material is based on a published article.

- **Citation is mandatory**: Even though you are the author, you must formally cite the published paper at the beginning of the chapter.

- **Re-write the narrative**: Do not simply copy-paste the Introduction and Discussion sections of your published paper verbatim into the main dissertation Introduction or Conclusion chapters. These overarching chapters must be re-written to synthesize the work as a cohesive whole, preventing redundancy.

Offense 3: Contract cheating (Authorship fabrication & outsourcing)

The doctoral degree certifies that you, the candidate, are the **sole intellectual author and creator** of the monograph's core research and narrative. **Contract cheating** is the act of engaging an external party—such as a commercial writing agency, paper mill, or individual ghostwriter—to compose any substantial portion of the dissertation and then submitting it as your own original work.

This is the gravest ethical violation and the most comprehensive act of academic fraud. It completely invalidates the degree, as the work presented is not an authentic reflection of your scholarship. Unlike standard plagiarism (theft of words), contract cheating is **authorship fabrication**. Discovery of this practice can lead to:

- **Immediate expulsion** from the program.
- **Permanent forfeiture** of the degree, even if discovered years later.
- A **non-reparable professional reputation** failure.

While seeking editorial feedback and copyediting is standard practice, the ethical line is crossed the moment an external party undertakes the writing or creation of the intellectual content—including generating text via AI models without proper disclosure, which violates institutional authorship policies.

Conflict of Interest (COI) declaration

A **Conflict of Interest** exists when a financial or personal relationship could potentially bias your research, analysis, or judgment.

Mandatory Disclosure

You must disclose any potential conflicts of interest in a dedicated section, typically placed after the Acknowledgement or at the end of the Introduction.

- **Financial Interests**: Did you receive payment, grant funding, or equipment from a company whose products or services are featured in your research? (e.g., a software company or pharmaceutical firm).

- **Personal relationships**: Does any co-author or committee member have a close personal or familial relationship with you that could be construed as influencing the outcome or review of the research?

If you have no conflicts, you must state: "The author declares no conflicts of interest."

By meticulously reviewing your ethical compliance, affirming authorship roles, safeguarding data privacy, and declaring any conflicts of interest, you establish an unimpeachable foundation of integrity. With all administrative and ethical checks complete, you are ready to transition to the main task: Synthesizing the narrative and writing the final dissertation.

V

Completion and launch- Breakthrough and beyond

You've reached the final arc. This section guides you through the process of transforming disjointed chapters into a cohesive dissertation and defending your expertise. Then, we look beyond the degree, teaching you how to translate your skills for any career path (academic or industry) and define the lasting legacy of your scholarly journey.

32

Synthesis of findings for final dissertation

This chapter moves beyond individual studies to fulfill the central requirement of the doctoral degree: transforming a portfolio of independent papers into a unified scholarly monograph. It is here that the scattered beams of evidence from your published works are focused, culminating in a single, authoritative statement of the research program's contribution.

But first, do you know how many kinds of dissertation exist?

Understanding dissertation architectures

Before you begin the physical compilation, you must identify the structural "shell" required by your institution. Generally, dissertations fall into two categories:

- **The traditional monograph:** A single, continuous narrative written from start to finish (Introduction, Literature Review, Methodology, multiple Results chapters, and a Conclusion). This is common in the Humanities and Social Sciences.

- **The sandwich dissertation (Dissertation by publication):** A compilation of three to five peer-reviewed journal articles or conference papers, "sandwiched" between a comprehensive introductory chapter (The *Exegesis*) and a unified concluding synthesis. This is the standard in most STEM and empirical disciplines.

Once you have identified the dissertation architecture that works for your field, your committee and your advisor, you are now ready to begin assimilating all your results into a dissertation for the final step in your PhD journey.

Why we focus on the "Sandwich":

Throughout this book, we have treated your PhD as a series of strategic publications. Therefore, the remainder of this chapter focuses on the unique challenge of the Sandwich Dissertation: **Synthesis.** While a Monograph is built to be unified from day one, a Sandwich Dissertation must be *retrospectively* unified to prove it is a single body of work and not just a "stapled" collection of papers.

Synthesizing the research narrative

The papers in your "sandwich" are not discrete, isolated studies; they are sequential stages in a unified endeavor. Thus far, as the driver of this project, only you can see this but it is now time to make the rest of the world and especially your committee see this as well. Your job in this chapter is to trace the **Golden Thread**—the logical link that proves why Paper B was a necessary consequence of Paper A.

The synthesis must demonstrate **triangulation**: how linking different datasets or methods (e.g., the simulation in Paper 1 followed by the human trial in Paper 2) delivers a more robust answer than any single paper could. The focus shifts from what each paper found to what the **entire body of work** has proven.

The Dos and Don'ts of "Sandwiching"

Combining manuscripts into a single PDF is an administrative task; turning them into a dissertation is an intellectual one. To pass the scrutiny of external examiners, you must follow these rules:

The Dos:

- **Do harmonize the notations:** If Paper 1 used x for a variable and Paper 2 used y for the same thing, you **must** use cohesive notations in the dissertation version. This is your last chance to harmonize the representations.

- **Do expand the Methodology:** Journal articles are often too brief. Your dissertation is the "archival record"; add back the granular details, negative results, and pilot data that the journals forced you to cut.

- **Do create "Bridge" sections:** At the end of one chapter and the start of the next, add 200–300 words explaining the transition. Why did the findings of the previous chapter necessitate the study in the current one? Take any chapter of this book for instance, the previous chapter sets the stage for the next chapter and the next chapter opens with why the current chapter is needed. This helps readers interpret the entire document as a cohesive story.

The Don'ts:

- **Don't duplicate the literature review:** If all three papers cite the same five foundational authors, do not repeat those summaries three times. Move the bulk of the theory to your main Introduction (Chapter 1) and keep chapter-specific reviews very brief and focused on the paper's unique niche.

- **Don't ignore the "single voice":** Even if you had co-authors on your papers, the dissertation must read as *your* intellectual output. Ensure the tone is consistent throughout- same tense, same form of speech, all throughout.

The Self-Plagiarism and Copyright Trap

This is the most dangerous administrative hurdle. Just because you wrote the paper doesn't mean you "own" the text in the eyes of the law.

- **The plagiarism check**: Most universities run your final PDF through software like Turnitin. If you copy-paste your published papers without a clear "Declaration of Originality" or a footnote stating, "A version of this chapter has been published in [Journal Name]," the software will flag your own work as plagiarism.

- **Copyright clearances**: If you signed away your copyright to a publisher, you often need formal written permission to include the final typeset PDF in your thesis. Check the "Author Rights" section of the journal's website early. We have previously discussed this at length in Chapter 31- Navigating ethical minefields.

Now you know the Do's and Don'ts of sandwich compilation and the essential plagiarism and copyright check. But how do you understand which paper goes in which chapter? Just because you published Paper B after A doesn't mean it follows the same sequence in the dissertation too. It could be so that Paper C comes after A and then B. Let us look into a useful tool to make this easier.

Tool: The synthesis matrix for mapping your contributions to chapters

Before you write the final conclusion, you must be able to visualize how your papers interact. Use a **Synthesis Matrix** to map your journey. In this table, you don't just list results; you list how each paper "talks" to the others.

- **Column 1:** Research Question (from the Intro).
- **Column 2:** Paper/Chapter addressing it.
- **Column 3:** Key Contribution.
- **Column 4:** The "Golden Thread" link (How this result enabled the next study).

This matrix ensures that when you write your final synthesis, you aren't just summarizing—you are narrating a deliberate progression of thought. With your chapter sequencing sorted, the last aspect to manage is writing the all encompassing conclusion of the dissertation.

Articulating the grand conclusion

The grand conclusion is the single most important intellectual output of the dissertation. It is the final opportunity to articulate the enduring theoretical contribution of the research. It should move through the following layers:

1. **Reiterate the problem statement:** The dissertation is a very lengthy and at times highly technical document.

To make it easier for your readers, make it a point to re-iterate the core problem that this dissertation set out to solve. You want your Conclusion to be standalone and not have the reader flip back through pages to go back to introduction for a recap.

2. **Core theoretical contribution:** How does the integration of these papers modify or extend existing theory? (e.g., "The research provides the first empirical evidence supporting the existence of Z mechanism…").

3. **Practical and policy implications:** Direct, evidence-based recommendations for practitioners or policymakers.

4. **The future research agenda:** Identifying where the conversation goes next. This demonstrates that you have moved from a student to a peer—a scholar capable of leading a research program.

The Pre-submission checklist

Once the written content of the Conclusion chapter is complete, your sandwich dissertation enters its final administrative stage. Before you hit "Submit" on the university portal, run this technical and organizational sanity check to ensure your work meets the highest professional standards:

- **The nomenclature audit**: Technical dissertations

often feature hundreds of symbols across multiple papers. Include a dedicated **Nomenclature Table** in the front matter. Ensure every symbol, Greek letter, and subscript is defined and that the units (SI vs. Imperial) are consistent.

- **Front matter navigation**: Verify that your Table of Contents, List of Figures, and List of Tables are perfectly synced with the final page numbers. A mismatch here is the first thing an examiner notices.

- **The legibility stress-test**: Review every figure. Are the axis labels, legends, and annotations large enough to read when the page is printed or viewed at 100%? If a reviewer has to zoom in to 400% to read a plot, it is a failure of communication.

- **Back matter indexing**: For a high-impact dissertation, a comprehensive Index is invaluable. It allows readers (and examiners) to quickly find specific concepts or terms across all integrated papers.

- **Consolidated bibliography**: A single, alphabetized list of every source cited across every chapter, ensuring absolute style uniformity regardless of the original journal's requirements. Ensure you don't end up with missing entries such as author names, publication year etc.

- **Appendices & permissions**: Ensure you have included full technical codebases, raw data samples, and the mandatory copyright permissions for every published paper included in your "sandwich."

- **The Declaration of Originality:** A signed statement clarifying your specific contribution to each co-authored paper, defining exactly which parts of the work were performed by you.

From document to dialogue

With the final PDF uploaded and the "intellectual contract" of your monograph signed, the heavy lifting of writing is officially over. However, your dissertation is not yet a living contribution to the field.

The focus now shifts from the written page to the spoken word. The work you have meticulously synthesized must now be defended in person. This transition from a lonely writing process to a high-stakes scholarly dialogue is the focus of **Chapter 33: Preparing for the final defense (Viva Voce)**. We will move from the rigor of the dissertation to the performance of the defense, ensuring you can verbally articulate the "Golden Thread" you have just finished weaving together.

33

Preparing for the final defense (Viva Voce)

You have managed the supervisor relationship, mastered your data, navigated publication, and survived the ethical minefields of academic life. The written dissertation is now a physical reality, submitted and awaiting judgment. The final challenge is not one of research or writing, but of oral defense: the Viva Voce (Latin for "by the living voice").

The final defense is a ritual—a rigorous examination designed to confirm three things:

1. **Originality:** That the work represents a significant, original contribution to knowledge.
2. **Defensibility:** That you, the author, are the indisputable expert on the work.
3. **Readiness:** That you are prepared to join the community of scholars.

This chapter guides you through the intense, targeted preparation required for this final assessment, shifting your role from author to defender of your research.

The defense mindset: From author to expert witness

The defense is less about your committee testing your knowledge and more about you proving your intellectual ownership. You must adjust your psychological state:

- **Own the authority:** For this specific, narrow topic, you know more than anyone else in the room. This confidence is your strongest asset.
- **Focus on the narrative:** Re-read your dissertation not as a collection of chapters, but as a single, persuasive story. The examiners are looking for the thread that ties the Literature Review, Methodology, and Conclusion together.
- **The goal is conversation, not combat:** While it is an exam, the best defenses become constructive scholarly discussions. Acknowledge valid critiques gracefully, but hold the line on your core contributions.

The pillars of defense preparation

Effective Viva preparation is built on two simultaneous tracks: ***dissertation mastery*** and ***simulated stress testing***.

Total dissertation mastery

You must know your document inside and out, including the location of every key piece of information.

Index the obvious: Create a **dissertation index card (DIC)** or handy cheat sheet that lists the page numbers for high-risk, high-priority items:

- Your masterful research question
- The core Hypotheses
- Your most significant p-values or qualitative themes
- The major theoretical models used
- The acknowledged limitations of the study

Prepare the elevator pitch: Prepare a one-minute summary of your entire dissertation, a three-minute summary of your findings, and a one-sentence summary of your original contribution.

The citation strategy: Review the literature that most influenced you from your digital literature review database. Be prepared to discuss why you chose one theoretical model over another, and why you excluded specific foundational works.

Mock defense and stress testing

Never face the defense without a rigorous mock exam but how do you set one up if it isn't a already a part of your dissertation timeline?

- **The mock committee:** Ask your supervisor to organize a mock defense with two or three faculty members who are not on your official committee. This provides fresh, unbiased perspectives.

- **Simulate the pressure:** Ask the mock committee to be tough, adversarial, and demanding. The goal is to stress-test your emotional and intellectual responses, not just your answers.

- **Record and review:** If permissible, record the mock defense (audio is sufficient). Review your delivery, not just your content. Do you fidget? Do you rush your answers? Do you manage the silence?

Anticipating the essential thematic defense questions

A successful defense requires you to move beyond simply answering questions; you must demonstrate **intellectual command** over your project's history, present state, and future impact. Preparing for these seven themes ensures you cover the vast majority of examiner inquiries.

Theme 1: The core contribution & motivation (Originality)

This establishes the **Why** and the **What** of your work. Examiners want a precise articulation of the project's purpose and its ultimate value.

- **Example questions:**
  "What is your study about and why did you choose to research this in particular?" "How has your research contributed to current thinking in the field?"
  "What would the field lose if your dissertation didn't exist?"

- **Actionable strategy:**
  Do lead with your contribution, stating it in a single sentence before elaborating. Always justify your choice of topic by citing the **academic urgency** (the gap) and **not** personal interest.
  Don't be vague; always frame your answer in terms of **new knowledge** or a **new method**.

Theme 2: The conceptual & nomenclature focus (Clarity of terms)

Examiners test your mastery of the theoretical landscape by checking if your key terms are rigorously defined and consistently used.

- **Example questions:**
  "How do you differentiate your definition of [Key Concept] from that of [Foundational Scholar]?"
  "Why did you choose to use [Theory X] over the more dominant [Theory Y]?"

- **Actionable Strategy:**
  Do know the exact page number where your key terms are defined (usually Chapter 2 or 3). Show that you made a **deliberate, scholarly choice** between similar concepts.
  Don't use conversational language when defining technical terms; use the precise terminology from your dissertation.

Theme 3: The literature context (The gaps & debate)

These questions test your ability to position your findings and defend the scope of your foundational reading.

- **Example Questions:**
  "How did your findings relate to the existing literature?"

"How did you decide on which sources to include in your literature review?"
"Which existing studies does your work confirm, and which does it contradict?"

- **Actionable Strategy:**
  Do treat your literature review selection as a methodological choice—explain the **criteria** (date range, impact factor, theoretical lineage) used for inclusion and exclusion.
  Don't simply list names; discuss the *intellectual debate* that your findings now participate in.

Theme 4: The methodological justification (Rigor, design, and bias)

This is the intellectual crucible where examiners challenge the integrity of your process, focusing on your design choices and objectivity.

- **Example Questions:**
  "How did you design your study and why did you take this approach?"
  "What biases may exist in your research and how did you mitigate them?"
  "What specific steps did you take to ensure the reliability and validity of your data?"

- **Actionable Strategy:**

Do justify your choices by referencing logistical constraints and the established literature that supports your approach. For biases, acknowledge them (e.g., observer bias, sampling bias) and immediately pivot to the **corrective steps** you took within your design.
Don't claim your work is bias-free; claim it is bias-aware.

Theme 5: The interpretation & generalization (The findings)

This theme requires you to summarize your core results and critically assess how widely they can be applied.

- **Example Questions:**
  "What were your key findings in relation to the research questions?"
  "Were there any findings that surprised you?"
  "How generalizable and valid are the findings to other contexts or populations?"

- **Actionable Strategy:**
  Do have your three core findings memorized and relate them **directly** back to your Research Questions (Chapter 16). When discussing surprise findings, use them to demonstrate deeper insight, not confusion. Anchor your discussion of **generalizability** to your specific sample and design limitations.
  Don't overstate the scope of your results.

Theme 6: The limitation & reflection (Scholarly growth)

This tests your self-awareness and intellectual maturity by asking you to critique your own work retrospectively.

- **Example Questions:**
  "What were the main shortcomings and limitations created by your research design?"
  "If you could redo your research, how would you alter your approach?"
  "How did your research questions evolve during the research process?"

- **Actionable Strategy:**
  Do frame shortcomings as **lessons learned** that have shaped your future agenda. When discussing RQs evolving, show it was a *strategic refinement* based on literature or pilot data, not aimless wandering.
  Don't try to deny weaknesses; acknowledge them gracefully and move on.

Theme 7: The impact & future vision (Practicality and trajectory)

This tests whether your work has relevance beyond the academia and whether you have a sustainable research future planned.

- **Example Questions:**
  "How can your findings be put into practice by practitioners or policymakers?" "Where do you see yourself and this research fitting into the academic community five years from now?"

- **Actionable Strategy:**
  Do discuss immediate publication plans (Chapter 26) and outline the next two or three research projects clearly. For practical application, use concrete examples: "A policymaker could use Finding X to design Intervention Y."
  Don't give vague answers; be specific about methods, outcomes, or collaborators.

Logistics and day-of preparation

The day itself should be about minimizing cognitive load.

- **Presentation mastery:** If required to present slides, keep them minimal. They are a scaffold for your argument, not a read-along script. Use high-contrast colors and large fonts.

- **Dress code:** Dress professionally and comfortably. Your presentation of self should reflect the gravity of the occasion and you will be presenting for a couple of hours, so your comfort is paramount.

- **The essentials kit:** Bring water, a notebook, a pen, and a physical copy of your dissertation (or a tablet version with searchable PDFs). Having the ability to point to a specific page number dramatically increases your authority.

- **Pacing the answers:** Take a moment before answering. A small pause shows you are processing the question, not simply reacting. Structure your response: **Answer, Evidence, Implication.**

The Viva Voce is the final, ceremonial acceptance into the community of scholars. If you can defend your work under scrutiny, you have earned your place. Preparation is the key to turning anxiety into confidence.

Regardless of a perfect performance, revisions are almost always required. Your PhD journey is not truly finished until those final corrections are signed off. Next chapter will guide you through the protocol for handling and implementing the revisions requested by your examiners.

34

Managing the final dissertation revisions

The viva voce, or final defense, is not the end of the doctoral journey, but rather the formal beginning of the final, administrative stage: managing the required revisions. Even the most highly praised dissertations require corrections, ranging from simple typographical fixes to substantial rewrites. Effectively managing this period is crucial for timely graduation and requires meticulous organization, clear communication, and strategic allocation of effort. The focus now shifts from proving your argument to flawlessly presenting your argument.

Deciphering the examiner's report

When you receive the formal report, the first step is a dispassionate analysis. Examiners often use academic shorthand that can sound more critical than it actually is. Your goal is to translate their "critique" into "tasks."

- **Typographical errors:** Misspellings and formatting glitches. These are non-negotiable and easy.
- **Minor corrections:** Clarifying a sentence, fixing a citation, or adding a footnote. These usually take hours, not days.
- **Major corrections:** Significant structural or intellectual work, such as re-analyzing a specific data subset or expanding a theoretical framework.

The Golden rule: Regardless of whether you agree with a specific correction, at this stage, the examiner is the final signatory of your degree. Treat the report as a mandatory checklist, not an invitation for a new debate.

Strategy: The revisions matrix

Do not simply start typing into your dissertation file. You need a **Revisions Matrix** to track your progress and provide a transparent record for your committee.

1. **Column 1: Examiner's original comment:** Copy the feedback verbatim.
2. **Column 2: Action taken:** Describe exactly how you addressed the point (e.g., "Revised Chapter 4, Page 112, to include the suggested reference to Smith et al.").

3. **Column 3: Location:** Provide the exact page and line number of the change.

This matrix acts as your "map." When you submit the final version, you include this document. It makes the examiner's job easy—they can see at a glance that you respected their feedback, which speeds up the final sign-off.

The final technical sanity check

Administrative errors are the most common cause of graduation delays. Before the final "Export to PDF," perform a final check on these three "Sandwich Dissertation" essentials:

- **The global search:** If an examiner asked you to change a term or notation in Chapter 2, ensure you have used a "Find and Replace" to update it across the entire document. Consistency is the hallmark of a completed monograph.

- **The legibility re-check:** Ensure that any figures you touched during revisions still meet the legibility standards discussed in Chapter 33. Labels and legends must be crisp.

- **The link check:** Ensure the Table of Contents and List of Figures correctly point to the new page numbers, as revisions often shift the text.

The win is a win: Pause and celebrate

Once you upload that final, revised PDF and the "Success" notification appears, **stop.**

The academic machine will immediately try to pull you into the next cycle of stress: *Where is the job? What is the next publication? How will I pay the bills?* Resist this for a moment. You have just completed one of the most rigorous intellectual challenges a human can undertake. You have moved from a student to a peer—a doctor of your field.

Take a breath. Reconnect with the "Why" you identified in Chapter 8. Celebrate this victory with the support system that helped you get here. You cannot run the next race effectively if you haven't properly finished the last one. Let the achievement sink in before you move your focus to the horizon.

Transitioning to the Professional Stage

When the celebration is over and you are ready to pivot, the "Scholar's Compass" is still in your hand. You are no longer defending a student project; you are launching a professional career.

The skills you used to master your dissertation—project management, evidence-based persuasion, and high-level synthesis—are exactly what will make you a formidable candidate in the global market. In **Chapter 35: The job search,**

pitch, and portfolio, we move from the archival world of the university to the tactical world of career placement, ensuring your PhD translates into the professional impact you deserve.

35

The job search, pitch and portfolio

Upon successful submission of the revised dissertation, the candidate transitions from an academic writer to a professional job seeker. This chapter is dedicated to the essential task of translating the extensive scholarly output into assets suitable for both academic and non-academic career paths. The dissertation is now not merely a document of achievement, but the primary portfolio piece that must be strategically leveraged in the professional market.

The big question then is when and how does one go about preparing for the next career stage? Let's dive into that.

The parallel timeline: When to start

A common mistake is waiting for the final sign-off to begin the job hunt. In a cut-throat, global market, the search must run in **parallel** with your writing.

- **The final year:** Your primary focus is synthesis, but your secondary focus is market monitoring.

- **The Final 6 Months:** This is the "Ramp-Up" phase. You should be actively tailoring your CV, reaching out to your network, and preparing your pitch.

The goal is to bridge the gap between graduation and your first role. Starting early reduces the financial and psychological pressure that comes with a "post-PhD void." If you are wondering- but what happens if I am given an offer but I am yet to defend and graduate with a PhD? The good news is that even if you are given an offer- Firstly, it serves as a security to give you mental peace which is crucial for your viva voce day, secondly, the offer letter will be contingent on your successful defense so, it's not like you have to wait till graduation day to enter the job market.

Now, with the timeline started, you must be wondering- where do I even begin looking for a job?

Reconnecting with the internship network

Recall the strategic immersion you undertook in **Chapter 22: Strategic work experience via internship**. This is the moment to leverage those bridges.

An internship is not a "one-and-done" event; it is a long-term professional investment. Before you blast out cold applications to strangers, **reconnect with your internship network**.

- **The follow-up:** Send a brief update to your former supervisor or colleagues. Share that you have completed your defense and provide a one-sentence summary of your "Grand Conclusion."

- **The internal track:** Many industry roles are never advertised. By checking in with your internship site, you position yourself as a "known quantity" who is already trained in their culture. This is the ultimate shortcut in a competitive market.

If this doesn't click, you can always prepare for a broader outreach campaign, connect with the Faculty you networked with during conferences, peers you collaborated with and look out for digital job boards. The next challenge is to be able to tone down your research for a broader audience so that you can prove your worth for the role. Here is how you do that.

Translating the research for different audiences

The central challenge in the job market is adapting the language of the monograph to resonate with diverse professional audiences. A successful job search relies on the ability to synthesize the core contribution into accessible, high-impact statements.

- **Academic roles:** Focus on the theoretical novelty and methodological rigor. Highlight the specific journals targeted for publication and the future research agenda laid out in the capstone.

- **Industry or government roles:** Focus on practical applications, problem-solving skills, and data management expertise. Translate complex theoretical concepts into business-relevant outcomes and impact on organizational strategy.

- **Teaching roles:** Focus on the material's potential for undergraduate and graduate course development. Show how the research can be broken down into engaging lectures or student projects.

The "**Elevator Pitch**": Develop a ten-second synthesis of your work that a non-specialist can understand. If you can't explain the value of your PhD in the time it takes to ride an elevator, you haven't mastered the synthesis.

Developing core job market assets (your professional portfolio)

The dissertation provides the content foundation for all required job market documents, but these documents must be newly structured and framed for professional impact.

- **The Curriculum Vitae (CV):** Ensure all three monograph papers are listed prominently as **works in progress**, **submitted**, or **published**. Clearly separate the dissertation itself from the papers, describing it as the foundation for the entire research program.

- **The research statement:** This document is essentially a concise, forward-looking summary of the Monograph Capstone chapter. It details the **single, overarching problem** solved by the dissertation, the **grand conclusion**, and the **three-to-five year research trajectory** that builds upon it.

- **The teaching dossier:** Use the dissertation's subject matter to develop two sample syllabi. These show the candidate's ability to structure and teach complex material derived directly from their own expertise.

- **The digital scholarly identity:** Ensure your LinkedIn, ResearchGate, or personal website reflects your new "Doctoral" status and highlights your portfolio pieces clearly.

The "permission to pause"

While the job market is competitive, do not overlook the value of a **strategic break**. If your finances and personal responsibilities allow, it is completely okay—and often highly productive—to take a month or even a year to travel, meet people outside of academia, and see the world without the weight of a deadline.

The PhD is a series of sprints that leaves many in a state of sensory deprivation. Stepping away from the "next paycheck" mindset for a brief period can provide the clarity you need to choose the *right* role rather than the *first* role. You never know which "chance encounter" in a foreign city or a new social circle might lead to your most significant professional breakthrough.

Transitioning to life after the PhD

Successfully navigating the job market—or the deliberate break after it—requires the same rigor you employed in your research. By strategically translating your monograph into a professional portfolio, you are not just looking for a job; you are launching an impact.

In the final chapter, **life after the PhD**, we reflect on the internal transformation you have undergone and how to maintain the "Scholar's Compass" as you move into a world where you are finally the one setting the coordinates.

36

The life after PhD

You did it. The dissertation is submitted, the defense is passed, and you've crossed the threshold into the post-PhD world. The feeling is euphoric, a blend of profound relief and genuine pride. But just as the adrenaline of the final stretch wears off, a new, more ambiguous challenge appears: **What now?**

The doctorate is a powerful launchpad, but it requires you to choose a flight path: the *academic track*, the *industry track*, or the *non-profit/government sector*. The choices are abundant, yet the rules are entirely different from the structured milestones of your PhD. This chapter prepares you for the realities of the professional world, helping you translate the immense value of your doctorate into your next career opportunity.

The academic reality: Scarcity and the faculty funnel

Let's confront the numbers head-on. The single most important piece of information to internalize after your defense is the shape and size of the academic job market.

The number of PhDs awarded annually globally is **many times greater** than the number of permanent, tenure-track faculty positions available. This phenomenon, often called the **Academic Pyramid** or **Faculty Funnel**, means that fewer than 20% of PhD graduates will ever secure a faculty role in research-intensive institutions. The job market is characterized by intense competition, temporary positions, and high geographic mobility requirements.

This isn't meant to discourage you, but to set realistic expectations. Success is no longer defined solely by effort or intelligence, but by market conditions, timing, and institutional need. Acknowledging this scarcity is the first step toward building a successful and sustainable career, whether inside or outside the academia.

Navigating the Postdoc path

For many who aim for a career in academia, the **postdoctoral fellowship** is the required next stepping stone to become a Faculty. A Postdoc is essentially a temporary, fixed-term contract—usually two to four years (depending on funding)—focused almost entirely on research, mentoring junior scholars, publishing high-impact papers, and securing external grants.

The joys and struggles of the Postdoc

- **The joys:** Postdocs offer deep, protected research time without the heavy teaching and administrative burdens that weigh down junior faculty. It's a vital chance to pivot into a new sub-field, work with a new mentor, and significantly expand your global professional network.

- **The harsh reality:** The postdoc is often a high-pressure waiting room. The pressure to publish frequently and secure grants is immense. Postdoctoral salaries are typically modest, often below what your industry-equivalent peers are earning. Crucially, the position is **temporary**, which can be mentally draining and complicate major life decisions. If you enter a postdoc, define your exit criteria—such as securing three specific papers or a fellowship—before your start date to avoid the **Postdoc Trap** of endless contracts.

A postdoc should be a strategic stepping stone, not a default destination. Ensure you know exactly what publication or grant milestones you need to achieve to make your next move.

Debunking the overqualification myth

One of the biggest anxieties scholars face when considering an industry or non-academic path is the pervasive myth that a PhD **overqualifies** you.

> ***This is a myth. A PhD does not overqualify you; it simply uses the wrong language to describe your qualifications.***

Employers in tech, finance, government, or consulting are not looking for someone who "published three papers on theoretical semantics." They are looking for someone who "successfully managed three long-term, complex, independent projects from ideation to completion," or someone who "designed and executed a novel methodology for analyzing multi-modal data sets."

Your PhD is a testament to skills that are highly valuable in the marketplace, but you must **translate your experience** into the language of impact, return on investment (ROI), and scalability that industry speaks.

The ultimate pivot: The strategic competency mapping guide

An industry recruiter scans a resume for an average of **six seconds**. They are looking for keywords, ROI (Return on Investment), and scalability. To win, you must stop describing *tasks* and start describing *impact*.

From academic task to business competency:

The Dissertation:

Academic: "Wrote a 300-page dissertation involving complex theoretical models."

Industry translation (Project management): "Spearheaded a 5-year independent R&D project from ideation to delivery, managing complex workflows and proprietary frameworks."

Conferences & Seminars:

Academic: "Presented at five academic conferences and gave seminars."

Industry translation (Stakeholder communication): "Delivered high-stakes technical briefings to expert panels and diverse stakeholders, translating complex data into actionable insights."

Teaching & Grading:

Academic: "Taught two introductory courses and graded 100+ papers."

Industry translation (Talent development): "Mentored and trained junior team members, developing standardized educational modules and quality control protocols for project deliverables."

Experimental Design:

Academic: "Designed a novel experimental setup and collected primary data."

Industry translation (Product development): "Engineered custom solutions for intractable data acquisition problems, optimizing data pipeline management and instrumentation accuracy."

The Literature Review:

Academic: "Conducted a comprehensive literature review of 500+ sources."

Industry Translation (Market intelligence): "Synthesized vast datasets and competitive landscapes to identify strategic gaps and drive evidence-based decision making."

Conclusion: The Scholar's Edge

Regardless of the sector you choose, you now possess the **Scholar's Edge**. You have been forged in the crucible of intellectual independence. You know how to learn anything, how to critique everything, and how to build something from nothing.

The PhD was never just about the degree; it was about the person you became while earning it. Your "breakthrough" isn't a single paper or a title—it is the lifelong ability to navigate any terrain with your own internal compass.

The sprint series is over. Your professional impact starts now.

37

Conclusion

You have just navigated the most rigorous process of professional and intellectual training known to mankind. You started this journey in the "Burnout" phase—staring at a blank page, a blinking cursor, overwhelmed by a sea of literature, and perhaps doubting if you even belonged in the room.

Today, you stand at the "Breakthrough."

This book promised you a **Compass**, not a paved road. It promised to give you the coordinates to navigate total ambiguity. If you have followed the frameworks in these chapters—from the masterful research question to the peer-review rebuttal and the industry translation—then that promise has been delivered.

The final transformation

You are no longer a "student" waiting for a supervisor's nod of approval. You have undergone a fundamental shift in identity.

- **From "Researcher" to "Strategist":** Your dissertation isn't just a book; it's a multi-year peer-vetted proof of concept. You have proven you can take a chaotic, undefined problem and engineer a definitive solution.

- **From "Student" to "Peer":** Your publications aren't just lines on a CV; they are your entry into the global scholarly conversation. You are now a creator of intellectual property.

- **From "Academic" to "Impact Leader":** Your ability to synthesize complex data and defend it under fire is the most sought-after skill in the modern economy.

The PhD scholar's charge

The PhD is more than a degree; it is a license to think, work, and lead independently. But a license is useless if it sits in a drawer.

1. **Stop diminishing the achievement:** You didn't "just" write a thesis. You managed a high-stakes, multi-year project with zero margin for error. Own that power.

2. **Trust the compass:** Markets will shift. Career paths will wind. But the skills you've honed here—resilience, deep work, and critical synthesis—will keep your bearings true no matter where you land.

3. **Execute without permission:** You no longer need a committee to tell you your ideas are valid. The world is now your laboratory.

Your journey, your map

You have the documents.

You have the pitch.

You have the unshakeable intellectual armor.

The master plan is complete, but the execution is yours.

Go out and own your PhD journey. You aren't just finishing a degree; you are launching a legacy.

And remember, if you ever find yourself in uncharted territory—especially in the complex world of Robotics and AI—you know where to find your mentor.

Now, go and execute.

Your next step: Sharing the PhD Scholar's Compass

Thank you for allowing ***The PhD Scholar's Compass*** to be your PhD self-help guide. I wrote this book specifically to shorten the learning curve, talk about the Unwritten rules and troubles of PhD and ease the emotional burden for future PhD students. But, the ability of this book to reach the PhD Scholar's in need of clarity depends entirely on you.

If this book helped you find clarity, confidence, or, a path forward through the wilderness, I have two final, vital requests:

1. **Leave an honest review:** The single most impactful action you can take is leaving an honest review (even a short, two-sentence review) on the platform where you purchased this book, especially **Amazon**. Reviews are the lifeline of a self-published guide; they signal to new, struggling scholars that this book is worth their investment and time. Your honest feedback is a map for the next lost seeker.

   If you have a moment, feel free to share it across social platforms like Twitter (X), LinkedIn, etc. When posting on social media, if you have read the paperback or hardback version of this book, consider taking a selfie (if you are comfortable) or, try taking a cool picture with the book and an iconic background to show where in the world this book is reaching.

2. **Refer a fellow PhD scholar:** If you know a friend, colleague, or cohort member who is currently experiencing the burnout, isolation, or alignment issues discussed in these pages, please pass along the name of this book. Direct, personal referrals are the quickest way to put a compass in the hands of someone who truly needs it.

3. **Share your suggestions:** Found something missing in this book? Or, anything else that could help prepare the contents for the upcoming editions of this book? I am all ears. Drop me an email at the email ID below and let me know what's on your mind.

Thank you for being part of this community.
I wish you all the best on your journey ahead.

Cheers,
Kshitij Tiwari, Ph.D.
Email: hi@kshitijtiwari.com
Subject: Feedback for The PhD Scholar's Compass

Doing my best to demystify and democratize the PhD journey

About the Author

Dr. Kshitij Tiwari is a distinguished robotics consultant, educator, and mentor with a profound passion for guiding the next generation of researchers. Born in India, Kshitij—whose name fittingly means "horizon" in Sanskrit—has dedicated his career to expanding the boundaries of both science and academic mentorship.

His own compass was forged through a rigorous academic journey that took him across continents over a journey spanning decades. He holds a Ph.D. in Robotics from the Japan Advanced Institute of Science and Technology (JAIST), an M.Sc. in Artificial Intelligence with a specialization in Intelligent Robotics from the University of Edinburgh, and a B.Eng. from the University of Hong Kong. This global perspective has provided him with a unique and invaluable understanding of the diverse challenges faced by scholars worldwide.

Beyond his groundbreaking work in mobile robotics and bio-inspired sensing—where his research has been published in top-tier journals and conferences—Dr. Tiwari's true calling lies in sharing his knowledge. He has served as a Postdoctoral Researcher at institutions in the USA and EU, all while dedicating himself to mentoring early-stage researchers.

His book, *The PhD Scholar's Compass*, is a direct extension of this commitment. Drawing on years of experience supervising students and creating widely-followed content on his YouTube channel and website, Kshitij has developed a practical, empathetic, and no-nonsense approach to navigating the PhD journey. He believes that with the right guidance, every scholar can move from the brink of burnout to a place of profound breakthrough and lasting impact.

You can connect with me on:

- https://kshitijtiwari.com/start-here
- https://x.com/drkshitijtiwari
- http://facebook.com/drkshitijtiwari
- https://www.youtube.com/@KshitijTiwari
- https://instagram.com/drkshitijtiwari
- https://www.amazon.com/-/e/B07V57MPZJ

Subscribe to my newsletter:

- https://tiwaritalks.substack.com

Also by Kshitij Tiwari

Dr. Tiwari is a published author whose work covers PhD advice, mentorship and applied robotics (field robotics). Below are other books that he has published.

Multi-robot Exploration for Environmental Monitoring: The Resource Constrained Perspective

Multi-robot Exploration for Environmental Monitoring: The Resource Constrained Perspective provides readers with the necessary robotics and mathematical tools required to realize the correct architecture. The architecture discussed in the book is not confined to environment monitoring, but can also be extended to search-and-rescue, border patrolling, crowd management and related applications. Several law enforcement agencies have already started to deploy UAVs, but instead of using teleoperated UAVs this book proposes methods to fully automate surveillance missions. Similarly, several government agencies like the US-EPA can benefit from this book by automating the process.

Several challenges when deploying such models in real missions are addressed and solved, thus laying stepping stones towards realizing the architecture proposed. This book will be a great resource for graduate students in Computer Science, Computer Engineering, Robotics, Machine Learning and Mechatronics.

- Analyzes the constant conflict between machine learning models and robot resources
- Presents a novel range estimation framework tested on real robots (custom built and commercially available)

www.ingramcontent.com/pod-product-compliance
Lightning Source LLC
LaVergne TN
LVHW010601100826
845148LV00014B/2800

* 9 7 8 9 3 5 4 6 9 2 3 9 0 *